PreScript: The letter is about to begin. One for the money...
A silence falls across the seats, coughing quelled, a cessation of
the rustling of programs. On your mark... The fuse is lit. The
curtain begins to rise. A brief hiss and the bottlecap clatters to
the tabletop. The conductor taps her baton and cufflinks flash arcs
skyward across the glittering flutesection. 1,2,1234. Two for the
show... Salad plates cleared, the waiter is approaching with a tray of
steaming entrées. Drum roll please. The lights go down. You strike a
match and cup the flame to the end of your cigarette. The opening
theme music begins. You finish the last word of the preface and
turn the page to the beginning of the first chapter. You put the
key into the ignition. Three to get ready... The machine whirs and
clicks to life, booting up. You press play. There is a crackling pop as
the stylus falls into the groove. Get set... The windup. The audience
rises in applause as the speaker steps up to the podium. T minus
five seconds. The referee points the starting pistol at the sky. And
go cat go... ...Go!

Dear Lamont I have been talking to you for the past three hours and I don't think you're really paying attention. You are four inches tall and sit at a small desk atop my computer gazing out the rectangle of sky high up in the concrete wall. Your unfinished notes from the last meeting of the committee on committee meetings are scattered across the top of your tiny desk and your tiny cup of coffee is getting cold much faster than my larger cup is. If I try to pick you up and hold you to the window will you gaze at the birds as they hop around pecking at the twine I have left out for their nests and admire their delicate aerodynamic properties or will you lick your lips like Wolfgang Amadeus Mozart, a cat I once had..? The way you are daydreaming reminds me of the time you took me waterskiing at the top of Niagra Falls. Neither of us had considered that the speed of the current might surpass that of the boat and for awhile I was quite nervous, skinny, knockkneed, clutching the bar as you gunned the throttle against a geyser of foam and we moved slowly backwards toward the falls with the rushing flood of water destined for gravity. Finally we began to move forwards inch by inch and then you turned from behind the controls of the boat to take a hologram of me in which the terror was etched in my face. Later over a dinner of live crab you were telling me about poststructuralism and I couldn't really follow how the transmogrified elementalism of postpsychic awareness had superceded a tendency on the part of all advertising companies to underestimate their audience's intelligence by an average of 50 IQ points. I think the wine is getting to me. I had wine, right? That was the time we were at the Virtual Restaurant and I had a Silicon Valley 1993 Binary Blanc and as I raised the glass of tepid water and saluted you you could not see my eyes behind the bulky goggles with trailing cables and electrodes wired to my scent glands, all of which created a low-resolution but convincing simulation of inexpensive white wine and a simulated wine steward who appeared to stand by the tableside appearing to wait to appear to refill my glass at random intervals during the conversation we had which I don't remember because I couldn't hear you because of the stereoheadphones with randomly generated synthesized clinking of distant knives and forks and conversations from simulated adjacent tables. Also when I looked at you the goggles showed me a yellow smiley face hanging disembodied across the table from me. Were you even still there? I struggled to get the helmet off. Was I even in a restaurant? I beckoned to the winesteward who bowed and disappeared in a flash of static. Lamont, where were you? Were you trapped inside the saltshaker watching me through the holes? Were you inside the peppermill hoping nobody would pick it up, your eyes and lips burning like the fire that had started between us, at the midpoint between Illinois and Florida on the border between Alabama and Georgia directly West of Atlanta. Atlanta is already burning. I hope the fire hadn't started in the trailerhome where you studied composition with Ligeti for thirteen years and where, when he explained how the technique by which he composed Articulations was different from Burroughs's "cut-up" technique, you got really frustrated and drove your motorcycle through the desert as a wake of coyotes ran alongside their long tongues flapping behind them like the unfurling paper noisemakers at your thirteenth birthday party to which I, incidentally, was not invited. Although I did get you a present. Well... I *made* you a present. It was a working ornithopter 100 meters long and together we sailed in it through the misty cirrus lit crimson by the sun setting over the Adriatic, both of us pedaling furiously, gasping and wheezing. Would we land in the water or pedal on toward a sun rising over Siberia? Over Siberia? We must have gone off course at some point maybe when, while you pedaled doubly hard, I walked out to the tip of one of the eight wings to have a cigarette. Which was not easy as the wing was flapping twice a second from your efforts. At that moment the horizon tipped and all I could think about as I fell through the night toward an unknown impact point, the lights of scattered Slavic villages like rapidly expanding constellations, was the time we met. We were in the same beer cooler at the corner liquor store. You were the barmaid on the St. Pauli Girl label, I was the distinguished aristocrat on the Sam Adams label. Although I, shy but distinguished, avoided your glare and secretly wished I was the devil on the Old Nick label, you exclaimed: "Look at this shit! The man on the label gets to wear a doublebreastedsuit and pose as if before a vastlibraryofleatherboundvolumes and is credited with theauthorshipoftheDeclarationofIndependence while the woman on the label gets to carry five foaming mugs at once while simultaneously avoiding being pinched by overweight nineteenth century Germans with missing teeth and smiling, and is referred to as the "St.Pauli 'Girl.'" And I don't even want to talk about the lazy Mexican on the Kahlua bottle as compared to the pristine Britishman on the Beefeater bottle. Which ethnic stereotype makes a smoother Black Russian? Hmmm?" I could not speak, I was printed in three colors, but I think you sensed at that moment that I was not brewed according to Germany's purity act of 1516. For the time being, that was enough to distinguish me from the monk on the Franziskaner Hefe-Weissbier label. And you from the woman in the Lite poster. That night we were bought by the same customer and ended up in the same paperbag, later in the same refrigerator. I could not speak but hoped that the woman who bought us would drink me first as I could not bear the thought of being left alone in the dark refrigerator with the partiallyconsumed roast, that way perhaps you would get to witness my opening. I was badly shaken and I knew it would be glorious. My head would erupt much the way it did this afternoon when I came home from class and the coffee was so intense that both my eyes were in the same socket. Rick had to hose my creativity off the ceiling. Then he called up your service and your beeper went off while you were stalking a panther in the underbrush. The panther dropped its briefcase and whirled around, startled. You emerged from the underbrush apologetically and asked shyly if the panther was an endangered species. Relieved, the panther picked up its briefcase which had come unlatched and you helped it collect its anthropology notes before they all blew away across the tall grass. The panther offered you an opportunity to live in its village and in the passenger seat of its landrover you thundered across the Savannah frightening herds of fleet elk which moved from your path as you held your strawhat down, your hair whipping across

4

your mouth. I never found out what happened but I got your postcard. It was handed to me by a mugger who had snuck up behind me on the streets of Manhattan while I was in line to get my weekly pair of tickets for the Broadway musical Rats. (I always saved you a seat. Even then.) The mugger took my wallet, put about 5 crisp V-spots in it, slid in a couple of creditcards (in his name) and bus tokens, then gave my wallet back and told me to put it in my pocket because he had a knife and might cut himself if I didn't do what he said. Then he said "Oh Lamont wanted me to give you this" and gave me the postcard along with a new CD player still in its unopened box. I figured you had put him up to it, and, indignant, I did not go to see Rats that week and somehow ended up in Illinois with my own theatre group. And I really wanted us to perform Herbert Brün's version of Cats "KaTzen" for you but your tiny desk was empty save for a few tiny poems stuck under the grain of corn you use as a paperweight. Where had you gone? I looked for Jean le Necre but found only a cryptic halfeaten note he had left. I tried to read your poems but the thin paper melted to my fingertip at the slightest touch, and the ink blurred, microscopic and illegible. It would have been much different if I had been a lego person and merely posed smiling against riveted backdrops. Plastic vehicles and the maintenance thereof, waving from behind the immobile handlebars of threewheeled motorcycles, operating painted computerdials on rockets fused solid with plastic. And those evenly distributed rivets on all horizontal surfaces... What are those? They're all over everything. What do you mean "that's how I stuck you together?" What are you talking about? Why are you taking off that guy's hair? You don't take off his **hair** to put a **hat** on, silly! Oh my God! He's got one of those rivets on his head! I do not! I have a spacehelmet. Don't touch it, I'll depressurize! ...You were hundreds of times my size but were very gentle. You held me high in the air in your cushioned palm and showed me how legoland ended about a foot away from where I was first assembled. I used to be a cowboy, you said, until you had taken the cowboy hat off and put the space helmet on at which time I had assumed a new personality even though my head, a yellow plastic smileyface, had always been mine. It was true, the sticker on the front of my blue thorax, above the seam where my own rivets divided my body into segments, was a crude western shirt simulacrum. It was not a space suit. My hands were yellow, not blue: I had no gloves. Why didn't I depressurize? Was your atmosphere breathable, Lamont? There was so much I did not understand. You set me on the windowsill and showed me all the other lego people, many of whose segments I had once worn with my head. You asked me how many men and how many women there were. I answered "two women and sixteen men." You asked me to count the people again. There were two with pigtails, one with a blowwave, five with messengerhats, four with medievalhelmets, two with hardhats, one with a cowboyhat, and one with a chef'shat. And me with my space helmet! "two women and seventeen men." You frowned and I wondered what I had said wrong when you removed the pigtails from one of the women and a hardhat from one the men and replaced them on the opposite heads. "now the woman is a man" I exclaimed. You corrected me, explaining that the head was still the same. "i don't understand!" I cried.... "They are all Women," you explained, "including you." This confused me a lot and, just to reassure me, you put me in the driver's seat of the biggest van where I smiled at you from behind the plastic windshield. It was reassuring indeed, being behind the immobile handlebars of the largest vehicle knowing that it was never ever going to roll anywhere unless, of course, you pushed it. But you had resumed typing by then and were staring studiously at your unfinished screenplay for the upcoming blockbuster multitrillion cinematic feature film. You waved me away, busily typing the climactic scene in which you, played by you acting as your own stuntperson, drive your Transam convertible from the tip to the tail of a large jet engaged in supersonic flight, hit the tail like a ramp and, just as the jet explodes—shot with a brilliant missile from the jet chasing it—the Transam hurtles seemingly forwards (actually backwards at one and a half times the speed of sound) across a brilliant blue matte sky, and you don your sunglasses and somersault from the car

6

just as it collides with the jet which had been pursuing you in a spectacular effect. You light a cigarette with your last match (which you will have to go back and establish by writing the second-to-last match into the plot at some earlier point) as you tumble through the sky at the speed of sound. Your parachute opens and smoking calmly you are surrounded by machinegun wielding helicopters who order you to surrender as black robed martialartsexperts leap from the helicopters onto your parachute and shimmy down the strings toward you, triple bladed knives in their teeth, you phone your producer to make sure that the musician you hire to write the soundtrack plagiarizes from female composers in significant proportion and call for more coffee but I have fallen asleep on the couch with the television set on and, to my oblivion, the President had, in the middle of the speech I fell asleep during, looked directly into the camera and, seeing that I had fallen asleep, gestured to the assembled audience of journalists bodyguards and bartenders to be quiet, and climbed directly into the camera and out through my television screen into my livingroom where he looked around and saw what the honest average taxpaying, hardworking-if-at-all, Democratic-voting-if-at-all, college graduate had that he could steal in a hurry and resume his speech before I awoke. He went for the new CD player and, as he unplugged it, blew a fuse and the TV went black. He was now trapped and... Huh? Well, you see I have special fuses which only blow out if too *little* electricity is being used at one time. Yeah. No. The powercompany installed them, I didn't have a choice. It's a drag, actually. No. Yeah. Remember that time you came over and tried to show me slides of your cousin's amputation and I couldn't hear when you were reading aloud from the surgical text because I had the dishwasher, washing machine, dryer, and blowdryer all going at once so I wouldn't blow a fuse? No? Me neither. Can you hold on a minute I think I have someone on the other line... All these things I told to you over the phone Lamont for four more hours until you spoke up, and with the abrupt inhalation preceding your initial phoneme I could tell that you were somebody else, somebody with the wrong number. What was worse was that the woman I had been confusing with you actually had me confused with somebody else she actually knew, and when I tried to convince her that she had me confused with somebody who might have called her on purpose, she howled with laughter and said "Steve, your exquisite humor has brought me back from the brink of suicide." "My name is William." She burst into laughter again. It was really awkward because by that time the phone company's secret police had arrived and were rapping loudly on the door. Did their badges glint or was that just me collapsing onto the piano keyboard? My phone bill wrote me an embittered letter that began "...I was payable in easy monthly installments but you never bothered. Now they are coming to take you away and I will be charged to someone else." May he strike a D minor or another related chord before they drag the maestro to their van. I wasn't sure if this was a good stopping place so I called up my editor Lamont and asked her how many lines and when we were going to press. She didn't tolerate wimpy writers so I tried to make good copy. She smoked Brazilian cigars and only drank the best whiskey, some brand no bar ever had so she'd drag me to the most rundown dives in town to end up drinking orange juice instead and telling me about the prerevolutionary journal she used to run in Havana before she was forced to flee to America, clinging to the side of a nuclear submarine. Once, the publisher of *Good Housekeeping* had, foolishly, engaged her in a fistfight. That's a long story though I don't want to get into that. It's late. Aren't you sleepy yet? No? Okay, one more, but just one. But you always want me to tell the one about Lamont and how she discovered a Unified Field Theory called Donut Theory whose announcement to the international scientific community was suppressed by the CIA when she was arrested and held without trial for... Okay, okay, I'll tell it, I'll tell it. Settle down. Well it all started in 1818 when a female astronomer named... Skip to what part? The part where Lamont staged an enormous protest at the Los Alamos site where the first atomic bomb blast took place later that same month and how the protestors were all held custody as, essentially, political prisoners until after the bombing of... Not that part? Which part are you talking about? Porridge and bears? Grandmother eaten by a wolf? I think you're thinking of a different story. Woodsman? No there's no Woodsman to save her at the end of this one. In fact, at her trial, she defends herself and delivers a now historical soliloquy on the responsibility of the scientific... Whew! I thought she'd never fall asleep. So much time has been lost now. Now, and as the ebony sky ossifies above a vortex of luminescent clouds, Lamont and I watch the surf roll in tendrils of warm saltfoam. The gargantuan golden ellipsoids are resting about ten feet above the crests of the waves and rock with their movement as if floating, as if they were very light. A triangle of green light emerges from beneath one of them and hits Lamont's forehead and she twitches and with a weird accent asks if there are any decent restaurants on this planet. I spring to my feet. "No!" my voice echoes across the waves, hits Mexico, echoes back and in its echo I can perceive absences: the sonic shadows of coastguard ships and drugrunners whose exact positions I am able to determine but by that time the golden ellipsoids have long since continued on their way and Lamont is waking up on the sand wondering what happened. Should I tell her? Is she unscathed as she appears or are there posthypnotic suggestions she should be warned about for example she might walk into a decent restaurant, there's a lot of good seafood down in Florida, and ask for a table for one and with the first bite of the appetizer, baked conch stuffed with puff of jellyfish, all of a sudden a latent microwave transmitter etched in her psychological coding kicks in transmitting a powerful binary signal indicating the presence of a good restaurant to a satellite which will boost the signal and transmit it to intersect the course of the ellipsoids and her lips part hissing static and all the lights in the restaurant dim and the maitre d comes over to see if everything's alright... Lamont rises to unsteady feet on the sand. She feels a little dizzy and wants to know where we are going to eat. I panic. Denny's? Too risky. "McDonald's" I announce. Her bepuzzlement in the moonlight reminded me of the faces of those men on the cover of Cosmopolitan. I don't know how they fit them into those dresses. They've got great bodies I guess. Just buying groceries makes me feel funny about my own body: gaunt drooping bone acidetched skeletal armature of tape and rubberband controlled by a pulleysystem involving spools and loops of thread fraying and badly knotted jerkily lifting spoonfuls of granulated sugar to my chipped and dusty teeth of dry chalk, my vocal cords rusty corrugated metal strips along which the tine of a jawharp scrapes raspily twanging. I grin at her and she drops the teapot and then your phone rings wringing you awake on the sofa. In the sudden darkness the President is silhouetted by the picture window. You cannot see his charismatic grin, he looks jaded and sinister with your new CD player, back in its box, under his arm. You yank the lightswitch three times but the electricity is gone and you may not be able to afford to get it back this time. The phone rings again. In a flash of lightning his hair is brilliantly backlit and his grimace is the evil smile of a demented economist as his tieclip glints and he sweeps his cape across his face leaping onto the balcony over down the drainpipe and his heels ring away across the cobblestones of the rainy city. The phone rings a second time. You look at your watch. A minute passes. The phone rings for the third time. On the sixth or so ring you will pick it up. In the meantime you can go across the hall to your neighbor's apartment and use her phone to report the robbery and order a pizza. If she isn't developing photographs or doing experiments with weird radioactive isotopes or glassblowing or working with liquid nitrogen or sautering or I understand she works over at the medical college designing a superadvanced sonogram that can actually tell you your unborn child's **name**. Knock Knock. Who's There? Lamont. Lamont who? Lamont who playfully bats the time/money continuum under the couch. The phone rang for the fourth time and the answeringmachine picked it up... It was William calling from East Berlin. Lamont sets the briefcase containing all the money down on the kitchen counter and stares out over the spires and cupolas of the windy village and the vocal timbres in the tiny speaker already reminded her of what he looked like the last time she shot him out of the pneumatic cannon and he tore through the roof of the big top and never came down as the audience jeered and threw peanutshells from the crowded risers. She had watched the ragged hole of sky with a tear descending at the edge of her painted smile, and honked once, sadly, in parting. The gears of the answering machine engaged and the tape began to record "Lamont Perkins this is William Gillespie calling from over here in accounts receivable. The other day we got a memo from you regarding stolen office supplies and I just wanted to tell you that it was incredible. The part about *routine searches of employees's desks* was really really moving, especially the sentence that said *if these measures do not bring the problem under control, more serious penalties may implemented* almost brought me to tears, I mean your use of the word *implemented* I think, rang so poetic and yet so true that all of us up here in accounts receivable just stood around the bulletin board saying nothing, holding hands. We were afraid to speak and when we sat back at our desks it seemed that time now moved sluggishly in the assimilation of every meaningful instant, discreet and intractable, I guess I don't really know how to explain it in words, I just felt like a babybird in the nest of the parent company and realized that the slightest breeze might send me tumbling, wet and ruffled, bare tail over underdeveloped wings, to the ground to be almost certainly devoured by cats..." "Hello?" You had picked up the phone interrupting me in midsentence. Something in your tone of voice set me off. As if I had cooked you chicken and sausage jambalaya with a side of shrimp only to find out you were vegetarian. Or if I had spent 25 years designing a perpetualmotionmachine for your coffeetable, only to be told that solarpowered didn't count. As if I had spent months on a portrait of you only to discover that I had painted the Mona Lisa by accident instead. "Yeah..." I finally responded. "Did you order a pizza?" "Yes." you answered. "You said you wanted twelve inch?" "Yes." "Okay—now is that radius or diameter." "Circumference." "Ah-ha!" In the background you could hear the excitement among the cooks who had been arguing about this measurement for fifteen minutes while all the other customers' pizzas burned joyously. There was the sound of measuring tape rattling back into its metal shell. There was loud quibbling about the value of pi, as

22/7 was not accurate enough for the chef. You hung up on this confusion and turned back to our chess game. I had all my pieces except for one pawn and you had one pawn, but refused to give up. Your coach shouted encouragement in your ear, hammered your shoulders, and splashed water in your face. I sipped liquid protein from a squeezebottle and tried to project all possible outcomes on a computer. Curiously, none of the possible outcomes involved a victory on my part. I called my lawyer on my cellular phone and exchanged hushed advice. The bell went off and you came dancing out of your corner, bobbing and weaving. It was your turn and you moved your pawn the final square to my edge of the board where it became queen. "Check" you said. The crowd rose up shouting all around the coliseum holding up lighters. You plugged in your guitar and prepared to deliver your third encore. And through the haze I saw that I could take your queen quite easily but it was your only piece and the balloons were starting to fall from the giant nets overhead as the audience carried you around the room and famous celebrities prepared to open envelopes and read the winner's name and the judges held up a row of 9.9s. You did a triple somersault backflip and opened with a joke. It was too much for William. He let himself out through a side door and walked down the snowy street kicking a pebble before him. The pebble snowballed until it was twice William's size and with all his strength he could only budge it inch by inch. Like that guy in that myth, you know the one. What's his name again? That's when he saw Lamont. She had just been thrown out of a bookstore for asking why the area marked LITERATURE was not instead marked MEN'S STUDIES. The tattooed bouncers had flung her in the snow where she now sat reading a stolen *The Wall Street Journal*. "They really butchered my article..." she muttered. William gave her a funny look and went over to sit in the snow with her. "Look," he said, "I have feelings for you which in the English language can't be given but only sold. So I'm suggesting we write a language together which is relevant to us." "Yeah, okay." she replied absently, skimming the editorials. William sighed with relief. Lamont looked up. "Wait, what do you mean?" "I explained to you that in a dream I remembered that I once had an older brother who used to sell birthday presents to me. He didn't just do it on my birthday, rather anytime Mom and Dad weren't around. He was a really insistent salesman and I guess I thought that's how kids played. I never told. Some of his presents were really, I later found out, not something you should give anybody. Years later, in high school, whenever a friend would give me a birthday present I would pay them for it. And every year my Mom threw a surprise party so I would be paying people back all year. Sometimes they got embarrassed. Other times they laughed and got used to it, and some of them even gave me presents all the time, usually something like old socks, and treated me the same way my brother did. I got really fucked up after that and spent a lot of time as a used car dealer. It's a period of life I still can't deal with..." Were you listening intently or tuning in shortwave transmissions from the Galapagos Islands? Was that even you I referred to with your name or someone else I grunted to in the first few words of our infant tongue? Or was it merely an improbable reflection of an unlikely idol with an octagonal bellybutton where the giant ruby was long ago pried from its stomach by Europeans? Was it all an absurd Trojan carrot inside of which armies coiled like dormant viral worms? I tried to teach you Latin but didn't know any. I wanted so much to explain to you the wonders of microelectronics and together we would kneel and build radiocoils with which to transmit our limericks to distant galaxies but I don't know how to do that either. I don't know how we could have been standing on each others toes the whole time, benumbed silent from politeness. I don't know a lot of things and someday hope to have written them all down in volumes of diaries with an intricate filing system of purely mathematical humor. Someday I hope to jump over buildings. Someday I want to strike matches on my tongue. Someday I want to be in a movie subtitled in Braille. Someday you will conduct the London Philharmonic and I will play all the instruments. When Someday comes, Lamont Perkins, I hope you are on my mailinglist. For you there will Someday be a subway stop in my ribcage with wheelchair ramps and expensive sandwiches. I am collecting all my silences in a burlap sack for you. There are awkward silences, cold silences, warm silences, contemplative silences, long silences, short silences, pauses for emphasis, are-you-getting-all-this-down?s, irritating silences, 5 second pauses, inhalations, and even filler words like like, y'know? Uh-oh. How did the ocean find us here? The surf is rolling, wave by wave, up the middle of the street rinsing a refuse of starfish and bananapeels and orangerinds through the gutters, cleansing the cities excrement from the bleached asphalt. Run! Quick, up these stairs! I've never seen tide get this high before. We were trapped on the top floor of Tallahassee Towers, the entire peninsula submerged into what was now the sea of Mexico, the inlet of Mexico, Mexico bay. Seagulls screamed by and people in yellow slickers waved from inflatable orange rafts where the tide was thumping up against the sealed windows two floors below. "Industry is extinguished!" one of them cheered and tossed us a bottle of Asti Spumante. I uncorked it in curls of thick foam acrid sweet delicate. People and sharks were frolicking in the water together, old differences overcome. Bathers in red suits hung onto hammerhead fins and were skimmed along the bubbly surface giggling. Dolphins knifed arcs from the ocean chattering articulately. I hadn't thought to call down to the raft for fine crystal and they were now lost among green and white sails moving across the blue. We slugged from the bottle, Lamont and I, until she fished a coconut out of the water which she neatly split into two bowls with a sharp blow from the edge of her hand. All morning we drank champagne mingled amid coconutmilk and watched Florida come bubbling, piece by piece, to the surface. I went down and raided the building for office supplies and by noon had dragged up the equivalent of a small office for each of us, and we sat at desks opposite each other, played with erasers, faxed each other stuff. Until sunset. Then we xeroxed each other's faces and wore them as masks. Remember? That flavor reminds me... Remember when I was telling you about the time Rick made chicken with rice lime and sweet coconutmilk? Then he expected everyone to eat it. He lay forks around the table. My face reddened and arteries bulged on my neck as I bugled certain vengeance. Well he is about to fall right into my hands. I just basted the chicken with the orange-ginger sauce and put it in the oven at about 350. He'll be sorry now, I swear he will. He will curse the day he ever thought about carbonara or stir-fry. When he comes home he will find soft music, dim lights, candelabra, and our best silverware—the kind that matches—all arranged artfully on fine linen with superfluous doilies everywhere. He will shriek a piercing shriek and, clutching his green knit tie to his tachycardiac heart, he will stumble out of the dining room into the kitchen where I will be waiting, grinning malevolently, wielding a chocolate cake with whitechocolate shavings and pistachionuts. If he surrenders now, and apologizes profusely, and offers to take me for a ride on his Harley, and whispers to me the secrets of the universe, and teaches me to play accordion, I might let him off with just a hamandswiss and halfacup of splitpeasoup, like the kind you served me the day I enjoyed waking up. Right now Rick is talking to you long distance about what he considers to be the weirdest part of Marxist economic theory: when capitalism is running smoothly, none of the workers can afford to buy any of the goods they produced so all surplus goods are routinely destroyed. Now he laughs occasionally as he listens to you talk about the 12tone Rave you threw where you cut your hand slamdancing to Webern. I can tell by the expression on Rick's face that even though he isn't going to say anything he doesn't agree that Webern was punk simply because he composed oneminutelong piano pieces. Did Rick tell you about Jean le Necre? He is a gerbil of distinction. He reads *Gerbil Quarterly* and wears a gold pocketwatch in his waistcoat. His artificial leg is of handsomely carved ivory and he slicks his hair back with the same enzyme in his saliva that breaks down the cellulose in the cedar he chews. What do you get the gerbil who has everything? Every week his linen service drops off a stack of freshlylaundered, neatlyfolded handkerchiefs monogrammed JLN. When the sun is out he reclines on deck beneath blankets and huge sunglasses sipping heavily iced Tanqueray with olives. At night I don't know where he goes. He grooms his whiskers one last time, doffs then redons his ruby beret at a jaunty angle, and is off to some gerbil club somewhere where rodents twitch in a strobelit miasma of primal synthpop drinking smoking choking on noxious exhalations from putrescent organic matter. Once he met a rat there who was the captain of a sinking ship and couldn't decide whether to stay on or get off. That was the smoke you saw around sunrise on your second day of circumnavigating the globe twice in a twinengine Cessna, not the one in which you skywrote your autobiography in cursived smoke. I guess what I'm trying to say here, Lamont, is that I dig you perhaps more than I can make clear with a watery verb like "dig." But what can I say? Everyway I say is boobytrapped with poetry and propaganda. I want to open my mind to you and point out the parts that actually work. Together, hand in hand, we can walk across the corpus callosum from my left hemisphere to my right. In other words, I'm so fed up with love being sad and sex being unpleasant that... Wait, that wasn't what I was talking about. This is how I keep body and soul together: I swig rancid maltliquor while listening to vile punk cello at maximum volume through faulty headphones.

I got a letter today from First Fascist:

> Dear Expendable Clientele,
>
> Our records show that your bank account has had a balance of one penny for the past year. This letter is to inform you that we are not a charitable institution.

and I called them up and asked to speak to the President and was put on hold for a week and when she finally picked up the phone I, weak from malnutrition, whispered "listen: don't do me any favors." I was pretty sure she wouldn't. So a couple of days later in the mail I received nothing from Tallahassee Florida but got an envelope from First Fascist and when I opened it up I found a check made out to me for a penny. So I walked all over town trying to find a bank that would cash it for me. You had to have an account. At the grocery store there was a twentyfive cent check cashing fee. Finally I endorsed it over to the toothfairy and left it under my pillow at night and when I awoke I had a penny to my name so I walked all over town trying to find a parking meter that would take one and when I did I stood in the rectangle delineated by the painted stripes and yelled at cars who tried to park there. It had proven to be a shrewd real estate investment. I finally sold it to some guy for a nickel. I should have held out for a dime. Speaking of poverty, Lamont you can be sure I would tell you if there was ever a time I had exhausted my supply of words for you. On second thought I guess you can't. I wouldn't. How could I? I couldn't. I would merely wheeze and wilt across these keys, my liquified musculature running molten butter into the sensitive microelectronic circuits. Soft sparks would cascade across the wind as dandelion fluff and you would smell my burning hair and realize that I had squandered my last synapse all to make you laugh. Is any of this making you laugh? If not send it back and I can for sure rework a few things. Wait a minute there's somebody on the phone. Hello? Hi Lamont, I was just writing a letter to you. Oh can you hold on there's somebody at the door. Lamont! Come in. I was just on the phone with Lamont, you two will have to say hi to each other. Oh thanks: my mail. Here's two letters from Lamont, and a big box I wonder what's in it? I'll open it. Oh my God it's Lamont! Oh I hope you sent yourself first class at least. Oh look at you you're a mess. You're covered with bits of twine and packing tape. How did you manage to tape the box shut, anyway? Wow. Well we gotta talk more quietly I don't want to wake my housemate Lamont. You'll like her. I think. Oh hold on, I'm on the phone with Lamont. Lamont? Can I call you right back I'm supposed to call Lamont. Thanks. Lamont, make yourself comfortable I'll be right with you as soon as I get off the phone with... Lamont? Hi. Did I wake you? What time is it out there anyway? Wow. There's a thirteen hour difference between there and here. That's weird. It's what? Moonlight savings time? Are you kidding? Lamont what's the matter? You sound really tired. Did I interrupt you in the middle of that dream where the pentagon has

Hewlett-Packard deliver a pizza to your house as a joke and when it gets there it's fifteen feet across and costs two billion dollars and the pizza delivery woman is standing on your lawn glaring at you with her arms folded and you wonder if you should try to run but you know it will be like running through honey? Not that one, huh? You only had that pizza dream once? Which one is the recurring dream? Oh wait don't tell me is it the one where you were elected president in a landmark landslide victory and you're tuning your guitar while dozens of sweaty aides try to talk you out of singing your inaugural address but you are calm and determined and just as you are walking out to the podium which is bedecked in garlands and flags the phone rings and you wake up? Okay. What do you mean "it's always you." Am I really the *only* one who ever calls and wakes you from your inaugural dream always at the critical moment? Gosh... Maybe I shouldn't call. What with the thirteen hour time difference and everything... Really? You mean it? Thanks. You can't wake *me* up anytime though. And anyway, why do you call it a thirteen hour time difference instead of an eleven hour difference? It's the same. Look at a clock. Hey, besides, how come there's a thirteen hour time difference when a couple months ago it was just one hour? Really. Florida and Illinois are moving farther apart? Tectonic what? Hey I don't know anything about that but I should really try to get out there and visit you before its too late. I mean, what if Florida ends up in the South Atlantic by itself, sort of in the Polynesian islands somewhere... Pacific, that's the one I meant. What? How should I know maybe it drifted through the Panama Canal, and um all the Floridan wildlife evolve unique strains since they aren't, um, whattayacallit? crossbreeding... I'm not explaining it very well I know. Who? Jean Baptiste Antoine de Monet, Chevalier de LaMarck who? I don't know any of that, but listen, um, like in Austria, I mean Australia, because its animals were separated so effectively from their genetic lineage on other continents there, there's, like, animals in Australia that totally resemble nothing seen on any other continent, like, um, koalas, kangaroos, Tasmanian devils, *two* species of egg-laying animals which are, um, I forget, um, oh yeah the shiny echidnas and the duckbilled platypi... Stop interrupting me. Well how was I supposed to know you were a biologist? What graduation ceremony? Oh, yeah, geez. Sorry about that by the way. Too much punch. Yeah. Um, hey is this an okay time to talk? You're not like, spotwelding or something. Sleeping? Oh no, did I wake you? I keep trying to walk over to your house but Illinois Kentucky Tennessee Alabama and Florida are in the way. Maybe if we each go outside and push Illinois and Florida toward one another all five states will compact into a mountain so high it scuffs the moon on certain days of the year and then we can dynamite a hole right through and build a railroad from your boarding platform to mine with stops for all our friends. It's worth a try. I'm going outside right after I finish this page and start to push. By the time this letter reaches you the Ohio river will run through my front yard. You see, Doctor, I get into these different states and there are special people I can talk to when I'm in each of them. I call them my "friends." Lately I've been talking to one of my friends in a different state than the one I'm presently in. I am attracted to people in different states. It brings out something in their handwriting. Hey Doc do you remember when we were black widow spiders? I was a male and you were the female and to be honest I didn't really trust you. That's why I avoided the contact of your multiple simple eyes. Scientists had put a drop of LSD on my carapace in order to study and photograph my webs. And if its true that the queen bee mates with the drone who can fly highest, selectively hovering above their clumsy swarm, then I am going to cool the hive by fanning my wings and let the others construct the honeycomb. I intend to do extensive damage to crops, yes, but I am still in the larval stage. After the pupa chrysalis I may not even feed, flittering away the energy derived solely from the fat stores I accumulate now by ingesting cabbage leaf leavening leaving only a fan of delicate twigs. I am not much to look at now, I know, but I am a voracious larva whose miniscule sluglike form renders him invisible to predators such as birds. After my metamorphosis you can chase me with your net. I will someday emerge from this dacron cocoon on wings of stained glass hinged on a thorax of polished chrome. My antennae will pick up police radios and telemetry. I will land on the window you stare through chewing the eraser end of your pencil, about to inscribe the last note of your first symphony, and eclipse the sun. Rectangles of spectrumedged color become parallelograms when I beat my wings slowly. This species of composer is extremely rare. Once finished she will tack the score to her wall and feed on "sandwiches" from the kitchen. Her crude but effective dwelling is primarily constructed from steelreinforced concrete. Her daycycle is typical of advanced humans. After feeding, the female instinctively reads until the resting phase. Once a week there is a ceremony where she stands in long lines to buy food. Her refrigerator is a special adaptation which enables her to digest this food extremely slowly. Her jointed fingers give her great dexterity. All humans want only to integrate the needs and desires of their species as a whole. This specimen, as is typical, redesigns her society every morning over "coffee." Her goal is that all human needs on every continent be unconditionally met. We have the technological capability, the abolition of capitalism and its consequent violence is imminent. Ever since President Perkins closed the military there's been a lot of surplus weaponry around. Of course nobody needs weapons anymore and are beating the nuclear submarines into solar power plants. Last night I went out drinking with a guy I know who owns a used tank dealership and later, when we were smoking espresso through a glass globe of water filled with tropical fish whose curlicue markings gleamed blue from his ultraviolet lavalamp, he got really mellow and showed me his AK47. Only its barrel wasn't tied in a knot like the ones on the brand new tanks he sold for about ten bucks a pop. I got really confused about his nostalgia and stumbled out to my car and drove for 44 hours until I got to San Francisco where I sat in Haight-Ashbury with a sign that said

NEED MONEY TO RENT A WALKDOWN
PENTHOUSE WITH A GOOD VIEW OF THE
BAY FOR ABOUT TEN YEARS AND A USED
IBM CONVERTIBLE LAPTOP AND AN IBM
PROPRINTER WITH 1000 SHEETS OF PINFEED
WHEEL FED PAPER AND TWO EXTRA RIBBONS
IN ORDER TO WRITE A GREAT UNAMERICAN
NOVEL AND FOOD

then I crashed in my car for about an hour and when I awoke it
had been stolen by you; you who had not seen me asleep in the
backseat. I tapped you on the shoulder and spoke to your surprised
eyes in the rearview mirror: "Listen, I can't help but feel that you
chose my car from the hundreds available to you because of
something special about it that nobody had noticed before, like
the fact that it has a dimple in the grille, or the way one headlight
comes on about a second after the other one, or the scent of its
unusually thick carbon monoxide." You responded politely while
making a left turn into oncoming traffic across four lanes on two
wheels under slippery conditions away from the pursuing sirens:
"Actually it was the fact that you had left the keys in the ignition
and the door unlocked and slightly ajar with the window open...
You also left it running. Which is not to say that I didn't notice the
dimple." you hastily added. Wistful, I reached beneath the drivers
seat and pulled out my 45 millimeter revolver which had been
converted into a semiautomatic Pez dispenser. I offered you one.
"No thanks," you responded, "maybe after I've crossed the Golden
Gate bridge against oncoming traffic at 88 miles per hour. By the
way that's the metric hour which is 100 minutes long which works
out to be..." swerving between two picturesque trolleys we
plunged down a completely vertical hill as you took your eyes
from the road to scribble calculations in the middle of the Diablo
Mountains on a tattered map of the bay area "... about 52.8 miles
per hour. Here, check my work." You tossed the map back to me
but I was staring out the window of the convertible at the police
car with red strobes barreling alongside gesturing desperately to

convince you, of your own volition, to pull over. Ingesting Pez, I queried: "Why are you stealing my car anyway? They're free now." We hit the exit ramp and entered. And in the hazy limit as X approaches an oncoming car I stared through the windshields and clearly recognized Zig behind the steeringwheel approaching opposite, eyes glazed in terror. I had always wondered what happened to him. All through highschool I was sure he would die young in some kind of freak auto accident. Did I ever tell you about Zig? Let me tell you a little bit about Zig. I am the hardest-working slacker in the lost twenty-less-than-zero-something generation X, but Zig is not. Zig has kind of a casual attitude about formality. Zig is determined not to make his mind up about anything. Zig is profoundly committed to ambivalence. He's pretty stubborn about being flexible too. A long time ago he decided he was going to keep changing his mind. He is the sort of guy who, in the 1980s, could smoke grass and listen to Cream and feel ahead of his time. He doesn't like to be told that he doesn't accept criticism. He is consistently random. He lives with his parents because he enjoys freedom. And because he can't tolerate businessmen, he works weekday lunches in an expensive restaurant. He waited on me once. He said "Hi. How are you this evening? I'm going to go get a pitcher of icewater to fill your glass and then I'm going to go get you a menu then I'm going to find out what today's specials are and then I'm going to get you some rolls and butter and then I'm going to see if you need any drinks and then I'm going to come right back to take your order then I'm going back into the kitchen to impale the ticket on a spindle precariously perched on a metal shelf above boiling lobster bisque (which is going to boil over) and then I'm going to make your salads my reaching with my unwashed nicotine stained hands into a metal receptacle from which I will try to pick out the lettuceleaves that most closely resemble the color green and arrange them on a plate and then I'm going to stir the salad dressing briskly so that the sheen of water is reassimilated into the thick orange paste in which ancient fragments of purple onion lurk within lumps of coagulated vinegar and cornsyrup and then I'm going to get really mad at the cooks who aren't going to even read the ticket and I'm going to storm out then I'm going to get in my car and going home I am going to turn on the radio and the disc jockey is going to say: "you're going to hear a couple of beer commercials and then I'm going to play a nonstoppowerhitmarathonrockblockwithcommerc ialinterruption which is going to last about twelve minutes and then I'm going back into the commercials so stay tuned for Led Zeppelin who are going to play, I mean who already played, 'Going to California' and I'm going to follow up with 'Going to Florida' by the Butthole Surfers-" and disgusted I'm going to change stations to "You're going to heaven, yes. You *are* going to heaven. If you repent _**now**_: it's *not* too late to repent now. And you *are* going to repent now. This is HOW you are going to repent now, my sheep. This is how: you are going to write a **CHECK**-" and then disgusted I'm going to shut the radio off and stare at the train going by. When it's finally passed I'm going to put the car back in gear and drive home and shower because a friend and I are going to a movie which is going to be great. Then I'm going to bed. You may ask: where is all this going? What is the opposite of going? I'm certain I'm going mad. Tomorrow I'll go happy. Sunday I'll stay home. And in spraypainting various crude apocrypha on cardboard circles in the backyard eagerly eavesdropping on the neighboring families I am going to come to the sudden realization that I would be less of a bad father than my neighbor because in forcing my son to toil pointlessly on an otherwise perfect and nondreadable Sunday afternoon I would waste his imagination with a task less like wrestling fierce weeds in the alley and more like spraypainting various crude apocrypha on cardboard circles in the backyard." and walked away. I knew he wouldn't be back by my table for awhile so I went to a payphone to dial your wrong number again. Because I had been dialing the wrong number nobody ever answered so I stayed up extremely late night after night trying you again and again. Because Andy was always using his modem to break into NASAs computer network (this was during the time he was busy sabotaging the Mars probe) I had to call you from payphones. And to avoid standing at the same payphone for hours, redialing your wrong number every halfhour, I rode my bicycle to payphones farther and farther away over and over day after day. I called you from a payphone in the middle of a cornswept windfield. I tried again from a particularly scenic payphone amid cacti at the edge of a steep precipice. I found one payphone in a cave. The only way to get there was by walking under a waterfall. I finally found out I had the wrong number when the wrong woman answered in the lobby of a hotel in Albuquerque. She couldn't hear me very well because it was Kareoke night and the hotel was hosting a convention of deaf rock producers one of whom was now rendered fearless by beer warbling a loud approximation of the lyrics he had never heard to American Pie by Don Henley I mean Donald Fagen I mean Donna Summer I mean Donovan I mean Dan Fogelberg using phonemes he had never pronounced while the other producers danced picked each other up across the room using sleazy sign language cliches and applauded the singer at random intervals. This woman seemed really interesting—she was a lawyer representing a hug insurance company which was being sued for redlining lonely people. She gave me your right number but wouldn't tell me how she knew it. It occurred to me then that I had no strictly academic reason to call you. Indeed, I was having trouble formulating a clear and concise thesis. It's embarrassing to admit this but I can't write long didactic treatises in opaque technical jargon riddled with graphs and equations. I try to hide it from you by writing you long letters of the silliest camouflage. I had a lot of things to write to you of critical and cosmic importance but I forgot them all and made stuff up instead. (see colorpanel #88) Sometimes though I worry: What if writing these happy letters to Lamont yields no happy letters from Lamont? Will her footprints be someday washed from my beach by thin tides of everyday foam? I will have to get on with it and write something new but what? I am going crazy because either my letter got lost in the mail or you've read it and are pleased or upset or both or neither and will call me or write me or neither. Maybe I have offended you for the last time and you are going to call the whole thing off and I will never again read your ballpoint or hear your syllables compressed in amplitude and pitch by the phone. The thrill is over the gone honeymoon. All gone said and done. Exeunt & curtains. Fine' & Ende. This is my stop where I get off. See you later alligator in a while crocodile. Don't take any wooden nickels I wouldn't take. Sincerely with all due respect regards love hugs and kisses. The end etc. Even if you shredded all my letters envelopes and stories and especially that horribly sexist Dr.Hook & the Medicine Show tape smashed into plastic shrapnel and returned it all in a big envelope postage due and had your lawyers call me to threaten me with charges of harassment by mail I couldn't just stop writing you letters just because I stopped sending them. Because they have liberated empowered and healed me and allowed me to paraphrase three words into a dictionary as a prism divides whitelight into a spectrum as a peacock fans its tail. But if I can't make you laugh then I will deflate limping and sag hissing my fingers will lose stiffness and wilt sending my guava strawberry juice to the floor asplashing. I can't make you laugh up your mind movies it all worthwhile it all difficult it if I try it to the top of the pyramid. Never wanted out with you you mine you miserable. So what letters can I write to someone who is longer reading them? I dip my quill into my inkwell and sign a florid signature. I roll this parchment up, cork it in an old Corvo Bianco Vino Fiore bottle, and throw it into the Mississippi River. My giant radio telescopes track your position in the sky rebroadcasting some of my most elegant algorithms in the hopes you will consider them evidence of intelligent life on my planet. Hmmm... If you aren't reading this then I'm getting desperate: how about that hundred bucks you owe me pally ...Hmmm? Remember? You had Vegas fever. You were on a streak. You were placing bets on which elevator would make it to the lobby first. Your luck held out. For awhile. At that point I was merely a bellhop in uniform trying to appear more like Sergeant Pepper than an organ grinder's lemur. And it wasn't the first time. I had waited on you before at many restaurants. You're always my favorite table. Your waterglass will always be spotless perfectly iced and full to precisely a centimeter below the rim.

Anytime you want to talk to me again just take a sip & glance around. If I do not appear immediately it is only because I am yelling at the cooks to bake more fresh rolls for you. I see you have abundant butter. Is everything okay? I will pillage the walk-in for radishes mushrooms black olives feta cheese, anything for your salad. My twentytop can wait for their separate checks because your primavera is up and passes my inspection along with the small pesto salad you didn't order but I thought you might like. Can I get you anything else right now? Very well. Let me know if you need anything. If only I could represent you in every branch of the service industry. I want to be the guy behind the counter who seemed nice. I want to be your podiatrist, shoe salesman, and the one who hems your lederhosen. Do you still play accordion so sweetly? Even though the little buttons on your Silvietto only played major chords you combined a C major triad with a D# major triad and the result was a stirring C minor and an E diminished and the dissonance between the D# and E brought tears to my eyes when you added a second tritone by trilling the F# which was resonant with one of my molars. "Toto I don't think we're in E minor anymore" I would mutter in low German and sip from my pewter stein until the foam soaked my moustache. That was on the eve of the invasion of Poland (which the author would be born on the 30th anniversary of) and while you fled to Switzerland and published a socialist newspaper I lived in a basement with other refugees. When I ran into you again it was 20 years later at a bar in Manhattan. I was the cocktail pianist and you were arguing with an important client. I don't think you even heard my precocious version of I've Got Rhythm in 7/8 time. Afterwards in my dressing room a few waiters came by and questioned my manhood. They wouldn't let up. Finally I showed them my beer and cigarettes and they went away, satisfied. From my window I had a perfect view of the crowd of photographers journalists and fans as your female bodyguards escorted you to your limo. Bulbflashes. Roars. A police helicopter`s spotlights. The blinking neon. I stepped out onto my balcony and swore a silent vow to someday find you a recipe for pasta that calls for ginger.

You see, I've eaten nothing but vegetarian pasta ever since the night I made white lasagna with mushrooms and bechamel sauce and the cashier was kindof cute so I bought two pounds of mushrooms one, at, a, time, and got to spend several hours in line admiring the way he moved the barcodes printed on the mushrooms across the laser scanner so smoothly he never missed. I wanted to let him know what kind of man I was so I handed him a hundred and asked for the change all in quarters, which I then proceeded to feed, one, by, one, into the toymachines in the exit vestibule, especially the one with the rotating plastic chicken which let out an extended cackle each time so I knew he'd notice. I had depleted two of the five machines and filled three grocerybags with plastic capsules each containing a disappointing prize and had had to call over a manager to dislodge a quarter ten times. Finally I stuck my last quarter in and twisted the knob home. The chicken cackled and the capsule that rattled into my hand when I opened the hinged metal flap had a ten dollar bill in it. I ran to the cashier for more quarters while my luck was hot. My hand shook as I handed him the money and I was wild and desperate enough to proposition him right in front of the Catholic priest who was buying whiskey but oh well. Finally two whiteaproned stockboys threw me out of the store and out came the bags spilling my winnings all over the mistencircled halogenlit rainbowsheen oilstained parkinglot. I collected myself and belongings. I tried to start my donkeycart: axles spinning splattering mud. My team: a cow a turtle and a beetle all on their backs. Did you ever feel like a spaceship, crashed and irreparable, smouldering at the end of the streak you plowed in the alien soil? Did you ever feel like an octopus tangled in barbed wire? A dolphin in a tuna net? Did you ever feel like... Remember that time the sun was out and you were flying me and I got stuck in a tree and you couldn't get me down and you climbed the tree and you shook the branch and you prodded me with sticks but all your efforts just tangled me worse? I was whipping in the wind my plastic multicolored tail fraying my delicate skeleton coming apart until I hung in the tree limp and flapping. Did your friends barbecue tofu that night? I ask because

I could smell it from the top of the tree. I stayed up there for months so happy to be freed from that damn string. I was home— finally stuck in the sky. You gotta understand: I want only to hang with clouds. Being flown was wonderful but being in the closet all winter was not. I still feel as though I owe you though: you spent so many hours getting the knots out of my twine. But getting stuck in that tree was the beginning of a new life for me. I had a great view. I knew everything that went on. I knew when you got your pilot's license. I saw you rocket overhead in that rusted Douglas DC-1 crop duster you got cheap. Once, you even dusted my tree with some (biodegradable of course) prototype magic formula. The stuff Tinkerbell was holding. I heard about the time your plane was pulled over by an FAA helicopter. Rotor light rotating, siren barely audible, it tailed you until, unsure what to do, you executed a crashlanding in a beanfield doing extensive damage to aileron and landing gear. The cop landed behind you and you sat in your cockpit for an eternity while she ran the letters spraypainted on your fuselage. Then she climbs out and swaggers through the kneehigh beans up onto your wing and asks for your license, helmet gleaming. You hand her your aviators license and she looks it over, nods, hands it back, says "routine check," and goes back to her chopper which has no trouble taking off in a cyclone of dust. Some scarecrow saw the whole thing and told it to a crow who told me, picking ants from my branch. By that time so many kids had tried to get me down in so many ways that I was a mere shred of fabric lashed to a twig. This crow never finished a sentence cawing endlessly and I just nodded, saying "uh-huh" "uh-huh" like I did when you extracted my wisdom teeth, pumping me full of... Maybe that wasn't you. It's hard to remember much and I've never had your hands in my mouth so I wouldn't know what they would feel like with latex gloves and dental instruments. There was a muzak version of "Dry Cleaner From Des Moines" with a muted trombone doing the vocals. I think. Again, everything is as obscure as the fog the night you netted the Loch Ness monster but, moments before the underwater photographer lighting crew arrived, let it go first classifying it as a descendant of Paleozoic-era

Holoptychius which gazed from its net with the same detached observation visible in the eyestalks of the lobsters in the lobby of the underwater restaurant. Because we were too broke to tip the maitre d we got a table without oxygen masks and after every bite we had to swim to the surface to gasp for breath. I often broke the surface at the same time as you, seaweed in your hair, laughing. Watching you through goggles already halffull of water, I was having real trouble squeezing the wine from the tube into my mouth and it kept shooting red jets of Beringer Cabernet Sauvignon Special Reserve 1986 across the diningroom. My tuxedo made it hard to swim and after a short time I just left my Mahi Mahi sauté down below, rocking on my plate with each tiny current, and stayed on the surface clinging to the chandelier. I had a great time. We treaded water together. The cocktail waiter swam over with blackcurrant Pina Coladas balanced on a tray and we just swam and laughed at all the other customers: elderly wealthies trying to eat through special oxygen masks while feather boas constricted necks, ties kept floating up. I was afraid being in the water so long might have given me wrinkles. Look at me, I look at least 24 or 25. If this aging keeps up by the time I'm 46 I'll look 48 or even 50. I am afraid I will experience momentary power outages which cause my programs to crash. I am afraid of losing my memories without you to back them up. I am afraid of rebooting only to discover that the floppy you left has unreadable tracks. I am afraid of being stuck in a dialogue with you in which I can't hear a word you are saying. I am afraid of playing handball against the bleached curving wall inside my skull. And losing. Your memory is staple, tack, paperclip with which to organize my files in this shifting irregular wind. Yet it is this wild inability to concentrate that has flung me farther from the corporate path than would have been otherwise possible. It is prevention and cure to me, it is pen and shield, it is attorney and landlord to me. I am not sure who I would be without it. Someone pretty dull for someone like me to talk to. The blood rushes like surf in my heart. It does not move as a river, it moves as tides. With each doublepercussion of my heartbeat my blood advances and retreats, advances and retreats, advances retreats leaving flotsam jetsam debris shells and tidal pools where urchins play. As I walk by a platypus delves underwater sensing threat of human contact. Paralleling your single line of footprints in the sand are a rut of my own confused tracks where I examined your every mark. I am familiar with the indentation your heel makes as it rotates on the point where it impacted the sand. I am familiar with the scoop it carves. I have counted your toes. I have read your letter. Never has a letter made me blush. Never has a letter made me tear up the house in rabid search of a dictionary in which, I eventually discovered, neither "teleology" nor "complicitious" was mentioned. Never has a letter caused me to slink under the couch with my tail low to the ground, my ears flattened back on my head, my retina wired to any sudden movement on my periphery. Rick tried to lure me out with primo catnip and that little mouse with the bell in it I like so much, you know the one, but in the past (there was, for me, a time before Tallahassee) my solution to all such dilemmas in which I have unwittingly aided in the routine slander of a person or a body of people I love was to simply shun the entire human race. By simply being biased against everyone I can be neither a racist nor sexist nor homophobe nor guilty of being the type of bigot I didn't list in this sentence because by not listing it I demonstrated an insensitivity toward the group of people victimized by that type of bigot making me one for example ageist—of my many unwelcome but inherent but changeable tendencies, the one I most recently noticed. With almost no acceptable prototypes, I am struggling to evolve into a man from a three-toed sloth (bradypus tridactylus). I can no longer let anyone read my first novel (short story). It is sexist, racist, ageist, and, worst, fails to be homophobic. I am ashamed of it but what is more important is that when I wrote it, with only the tiniest realization of the scope of my responsibility as a writer, I was really proud of it and waved it in the air over my head and cheerily gave copies to anyone who made eye contact and never stuck around to see them recoil in revulsion. It was a torch whose flame is still burning on the torch I carry now. I put my torch in an asbestos envelope lick it shut and put it in the mail to you. Do you open it with oven mitts? If I hadn't plunged blindly through the stupidity I would never have made it this far. I would still be in 1988 watching television, paperweight of the mind. There was this band called the XRay Spex who had this song called "Oh Bondage Up Yours!" in which Polly Styrene, the female vocalist, belted out the following words in a voice whose sincerity (and note) was impossible to fathom—it suffices to say that it was an enthusiastic message: "Some people think that little girls should be seen and not heard but I think: Oh Bondage Up Yours. Buy me Tie me Chain me to the wall I wanna be a victim to you all..." and I couldn't for the life of me figure out if, in presenting a horrifyingly submissive text and reinforcing standards of violence against women she was attacking them violently enough to make up for re-establishing them and if violence could in fact be attacked, and the answers to these questions interested me because I first listened to the XRay Spex in order to find more rock songs by women. However: the answers to these questions won't get me any farther than another rock song with the same rhythm and probability of a surprising chord as all the other rock songs whose only difference is the voice of the person who fails to sing it and the cool saxophone. How can I tell you this? I want to be the woman while you be the man: I'll be Tinkerbell you be Peter Pan. You could interrupt me, fail to introduce my to your friends, dismiss my ideas, refer to me with condescending monikers referring to youth animals and my appearance, act as though all my emotions are symptoms of hysteria or menstruation, explain economics to me with harsh unclear impatient descriptions, put me on a pedestal, watch wrestling matches or discuss philosophy while I cook a elaborate vegetarian dinner for your friends which they will reject in favor of hamburgers, accept credit for my childrearing with a smug glow of authorship, or even say that it is time my gender solved all the problems your gender has instilled throughout the centuries by electing me to offices in your existing hierarchy in order to justify your continuing oppression of me with this staged failure. But please do not rape me as adult child lover friend or stranger. With your assistance I would like to try on a woman's skin. My bones are pliable: you could decrease my shoulderspan, shorten my ribcage, and widen my pelvic opening. But even then there is so much else I do not have. Perhaps we can be a woman together for awhile until I get the hang of it. I could easily be the skeletal, digestive and muscular systems if you could be the more challenging circulatory and nervous systems as well as the skin and hair. Eventually, as I learned the cords, you would merely assume the role of brain and I would do all the rest. Often jaded, seldom callused. Christ was pissed: she'd been up there all this time and nobody had counted her ribs. Nobody had noticed that her beard was painted on. Nobody had noticed the airbrushing. Clearly, by this point in the letter its author was having a second crisis of faith. This letter, it seemed to him, could no longer really be called a letter. Its structure so far involved a series of improbable friendships between the two protagonists. O! Indeed, the author mused as lavender petals blew across the keyboard in the breeze of fluttering muse wings, this letter seemed to establish every possible friendship between the two characters except the friendship that existed between the two people after whom the characters were named. The events of the friendship had barely begun while the letter had long since padded off into obscure senility, the reflexive synaptic twitchings of an experienced writer with a fun ethic which was getting in the way by obstructing content. What content? The friendship consisted of this sentence, the one he is writing now, and its function in the larger composition of the letter. What composition? This letter rode the choppy contours of his only therefore favorite language: American 1993—a ruthlessly polished by poets and bleached by advertisers bastardization of a quaint antiquated and inefficient Anglo-Saxon tongue of Teutonic descent. The only modification the author inflicts upon the language with any consistency in this letter is to clump nounphrases together in a method he learned from studying German (in which, of course, Nounphrases are Capitalized). The English language's primary justification for generating nonhyphenated compound words is when the first word does not modify the second word but indicates that it refers to something else (floorplan is not a normal plan, bedpan is not a normal pan). The author's secondary justification is in noun phrases which are articulated like one word: when the second word has no stressed syllables (mailinglist, dogfood, chessgame). This clumping identifies the nounphrases as one unit of syntax: policecardoor is three nouns referring to one object, one figureofspeech. Ratsalwaysdesertasinkingship is one thought, one word. Acaptainalwaysgoesdownwithhership is one thought, one word. This is the fitting and proper way to deflate these useless contours built into everyday thought. Did you notice that there are several figuresofspeech in our language which have to do with travelling longdistances in woodensailingships, an experience those of us who use this language will, forthemostpart, never have. These rotting baroque wisdoms survived the passage from Britain by referring to it. Singlehandedly usually means doublehandedly at least. And what about You can lead a deadlooking gift horse to the mouth of a stream, but you can't beat it? Who has horses anymore? Furthermore the finest writing is consistently ruined by the use of the generalization Man. Through compositional techniques the author wants to alter syntax by transmitting English through different lenses (20 consonant writing for one) in order to understand its structure and functions (existing and possible) more clearly. In the composition entitled *Letter to Lamont* one method he has toyed with without so far understanding very clearly is the Point of View Transfer. This can be used to shift the perspective from which a scene is being witnessed. Essential to the technique thus far is transferring the point of view to an inanimate object, an abstraction, a very large scale, a very small scale, and through selfreflexivity revealing the scene as a scene. This is done by using first and second person pronouns with unusual antecedents. This can be tiring to read but has unexplored and interesting possibilities. The mechanics by which the transfer is made are infinite in their permutations. The film *Slacker*, written and directed by Richard Linklater, is an excellent example of a particular type of transfer. In *Slacker*, the transfer from one point of view to another happens when the characters are in the same place. The camera continually loses interest in its subject and follows another, and none of these subjects ever reappear. In the film, the point of view is not subjective (the camera showing us what one of the characters is seeing rather than showing the character) except when the scene is obviously filmed with a handheld camera. Even then the scene functions as a scene within a scene. As if the author had written about Lamont in the third person, rather than written to her in the second person. As the author himself ruminates: "The point of view transfer is very hard to narrow down to a definition. So I aim to in this letter to begin to make deliberate experiments to understand it better. I will try to make it clear what these experiments are so in reading this you can understand that it is not only a letter to you from me, it is a letter for you and me because I will learn from the experiments as I continue to try to paraphrase my personality for your entertainment." This problem seems to have perplexed the author since his earliest childhood efforts. What follows are a series of letters to and from Lamont written and confiscated in the third grade:

Lamont: I will be class clown for you. You will struggle to ignore me as I surreptitiously or obviously throw the class into hysteria and Teach into tantrums and tears. I will martyr myself a silly person. I will be sent to the office and try to catch your eye on the way out. I will return once to flatten my face against the window briefly, a virtuosic encore to an audience who is swooning with giggles sugarfits and insurrections. All except you, staring at your book, fuming. Why am I so desperate to crack you up?

William: Perhaps I would have appreciated your fart noises
more had they not been timed to interrupt my bold rejection
of the scene in which Huckleberry Finn attempts to assume the
mannerisms of a woman and fails because he can catch. I was
trying to make an important point and, as the laughter did not
subside for a full five minutes, couldn't. I despise you.

Lamont: Tonight you will shake my spitballs from your hair. Admire their craftsmanship: carefully manicured from spiral notebook trimmings and my finest saliva.

William: The tack you left on my seat may have been misconstrued by the squalid malfunctioning of your stunted intelligence as a gesture of affection, but to me it was misogyny. Understand: I am already in the position, by virtue of my womanhood, of being ignored or bullied by the boys and being ignored or condescended to by the instructor—a true dweeb imbecile and coward. My papers are five pages to your one with zero misspelllings and I have yet to get an A—or even constructive criticism—on any of them. Maybe you think this is funny. Maybe you are unable to grasp the fact that you cannot score lower than a B because your father is mayor and this has already cost you your education.

Lamont: I thought it was really funny when I got you caught passing your last note to me. I will always remember the teacher's face when he tried to read the word "dweeb" out loud to the class. It is the first snow of winter and you are more beautiful than ever. It is good packing snow. Be careful walking home.

William: By the time you read this note it will be too late to do anything about the firecrackers in your desk. There is no fuse you can cut as I have installed a radio detonator. That's right. Don't even try to raise your hand or open your mouth or I'm pressing the button. First I'm going to watch you sweat. Please believe me when I tell you that if I thought it was possible to reason with you I would not have sunk to just above your level. But when you said "girls are dumb" I gave up. I think you're kind of cute for a boy and it is almost a shame that your pretty, shall I say, girlish eyes will soon be bandaged over several times. Bye!

Now let us examine a sample of the letters written in the author's early twenties. Notice, in particular, how the imminent collapse of the institution of heterosexuality has caused the author to struggle against the poisonous convention of "l★veletter:"

It is May and Spring is finally rooted and blooming a preposterous assemblage of succulent colors aromas and textures sounds and probably flavors and Rick and I are holding office hours in an office consisting of a table two chairs green sky blue lawn neighbors and violet lavender lilac marigold tulip chrysanthemum azalea snapdragon rose, anyway the birds seem pleased with the way things are turning out of buds of sepals of the ground the bees are drunk with nectar and dusted with yellow pollen and buzzing swerve clumsily to different pistils between dandelions explode in clouds of fluffy elaborate parachutes transmit genetic information downwind everything is exploding in fertility and gaudy courtship as squirrels chase each other around and around the trunk their intertwined paths a doublehelix as they frolic for survival unlike me and speaking as a pair of ragged claws who occasionally scuttles across the floors of silent seas this time of year I see many a couple on a curb rationalizing their emotions in pleading drunken syllables when they are forced by circumstances to talk about their sexual relationship for the first time so out of loneliness I have arguments with myself and then make up and have great sex but there are still places on my back it is physically impossible for me to scratch and as I roll through the basilpatch trying a cop car drives through the backyard slowly so I will act cool and resume typing in this office in the sun where I can get a perfect tan by shifting my computer to another side of the table every thirty minutes which is I figure about the time it will take to finish this page and then I can tell people I got tan playing sports outdoors and they will give me a look that doesn't say "what a waste of time" but which instead says "what a productive waste of time" but it is a beautiful day after a grey winter and I am going to exploit it by intervening militarily supposedly on its behalf and then in order to assume control of its mining manufacturing agriculture and drug industries I will install my military base which is as I may have mentioned a cardtable in the backyard with a laptop on its lap and a battered extension cord snaking orange rubber through green grass in the door down the stairs into the basement and into an outlet in the base of a lightsocket which is starting to worry me because it gives me a shock everytime I touch it. Living in Rick's basement is occasionally worrisome. It will do until I decide to take some responsibility in this world. Someday I will go out into the world and look for a place to pay rent. But for now I've got a letter to write. Someday I'd like to settle down and have cats again. But plants make me uncomfortable. I never know what to say to them. Once I read the complete works of Gertrude Stein to a hanging spider plant. It took about a month to get through everything and although the effects were apparent—it grew—it never told me how it liked my performance of the piece. It merely groped for sunlight with imperceptibly slow movements. Plants make me uncomfortable. Someday I'd like to have cats again but for now it is enough to slide down rainbows. Now it is enough to ride clouds. It is enough to cup my hands around the sun and cast shadow animals across the tropics. Is enough too much? "Enough is enough," you say, "Nobody slides down rainbows. The hyperbolic acceleration would result in a fatal collision with the pot of gold. Few have successfully rappelled down a rainbow. Nowadays most rainbows have elevators that ascend jerkily like the one in the St.Louis Arch which traumatized you at an early age, instilling recurrent dreams in which an elevator gets stuck between floors and turns onto its side forcing you and the other passengers to stand wordlessly on the ledge of buttons beside the sliding door which you pray will not open revealing the shaft yawning beneath you and eventually the elevator turns a full revolution and you finally get the doors open revealing the fourteenth floor at an angle halfway up the door but luckily you can crawl out and stop by the music building steno pool to drop off a few scores and forge Schoenberg's signature." I agree. Last time I went there it was secretary week and I found an ad hoc team of administrators and faculty frenetically copying things. Astounded I asked the ad hoc team of administrators and faculty "but who are you copying things for?" The ad hoc team of administrators and faculty replied in unison "the secretaries! This week they have taken over all the administrative and faculty positions and are teaching our classes! They've already begun to institute surprising changes! They are abolishing the distinction between University employees to the point that former professors will sweep floors once a week and former janitors will deliver lectures once a week! This possibility has caused a run on the library by all the formerly nonacademic staff who are eager to begin research for their classes and the number of patrons is so astronomical that the former President of the University, who today is working as a Library Hourly, will be completely exhausted when she gets back to the dormroom she is housed in for the night (Sharing it, incidentally, with the former guy who cleans the giant anteater cages in the Natural Sciences building!)!" That night I found out I had the former President's former mansion all to myself. I called you up to see if you wanted to come over but there wasn't an adequately rapid means of transportation at your disposal as you couldn't afford to charter a jet. I asked you what the speed of sound was. I caught the hesitation in your breath before your reply: "344 m$\star$s^{-1}." Coyly I queried "well... how many kilometers are in a mile?" There was a pause before you answered "I don't know." I think you knew but had guessed my intention; that you should drive your car with the plastic BigBird hanging from the rearview mirror at the speed of sound rupturing the asphalt and sucking other cars into the ditch from the vacuum in your wake. Who was I kidding. Not only would it require incredible acceleration to travel at speeds upwards of mach one and still follow the jagged contours of the highway but I wasn't former faculty or even former staff, merely former student. I walked around the swimmingpool in the former President's kimono sipping the former President's sparkling blue kiwi kumquat water and mused to the moon amid chlorine fumes. I thought back with bittersweet regret to the time I had given you hanging ceramic planter earrings as a Commemoration of the Extinction of the Dodo Day (Observed) present and you never wore them, and I realized for the first time how painful they would have been. The reflection of the marble lionesses in

the shimmering pool was lulling me into uncertain tranquility. I felt weak as if years of drought and malnutrition had resulted from the routine torching of croplands by my warring peoples. All my existing progress in arts and sciences had been pillaged and destroyed. I may never be arable again. I stood beside the deep end and prayed for rain. The wind whipped a shroud of topsoil over the moonlight and my eyes began to water. I walked out to the edge of the 344 m highdive and considered a cannonball but in my grief could not remember how many meters were in a yard. Suddenly the phone rang and my burgundyglass fell from my hand and one second later became three seemingly distinct phenomena:
1. a delicate splash and
2. rapidly widening concentric circles etched with refracted incandescence from the underwater bulbs in whose centers
3. underwater clouds of inky blue juice billowed. And yet were not these three elements of a single system?
4. The phone, a seemingly distinct phenomena, rang again. What if it was you calling back? There was only one way to get to the phone in time: a graceful swandive. So I climbed back down the ladder as quickly as I could, slipping on silk. I made it back onto the deck by the twentyninth ring kimono tattered and picked up the cordless phone lying on the bar. I tried to exhale the word hello but could only gasp. I tried gesturing frantically at the phone, sign language, semaphore, writing it notes. I lay it on the glass tabletop and tapped out in pencil the morsecode for hello ★★★★ ★ ★-★★ ★-★★ —-. I put the phone to my forehead and channeled furiously furrowing. Finally the voice on the other end spoke. It wasn't for me. I hung up. I don't see what's so wrong with that. I guess I'll be a student for awhile. Butterfly get back into that cocoon! What happens if I try to think now? My gears are soft. I was listening to that Muppets I taped off of you and I specifically heard Kermit say "you jerk" in one of his songs. I think the one called "you human jerk." I had penciled in an extra hour of exercise tonight and, somewhat infuriated that when I taped it from you you didn't warn me but I guess you have a lot of albums whose entire cast is composed of furry monochrome animals with

39

googley eyes hinged hemispherical lowerjaws and bulbous felt noses whose thin upperlimbs are more often than not supported by almost invisible rods, I ran at an unsustainable speed depleting my renewable resources. I felt like a dozen white male puppeteers were leaning out of trucks on either side frantically manipulating the segments of my limbs with long poles with of course a camera assembly and lighting and as I plunged through the wet cut grass of simulated natural settings I did inexcusable damage to my left vastus lateralis in my efforts to run through the rain faster than any living male American of mostly Anglo-Saxon heritage prairie poet who grew up in a house whose attic he never saw because the trapdoor was in the ceiling of whose parents' closet and their clothes would be covered with the soot that invariably rained down if who opened it or so they told whom but who could still dream and that was probably far more interesting and who had a room with a large closet with a window which offered a view of the park in which other living male American children of Anglo-Saxon heritage played Basketball until about nine and then who had it to whoself after that ever had. Pop radio had made me nostalgic and I sat in that window like a gamete on a microscope slide. I think you were looking down at me but it was really hard to tell because through the wrong end of that microscope you were a parsec away. What has happened? I still play your tape but I can no longer hear it. My ears are filled with the rushing of the Gulf of Mexico which has extended a pseudopod to Illinois to reclaim me. Waves crash along the California street beach. I can't hide in the basement. I'll have to finish the attic in a hurry. Quickly I grabbed the phone and ordered some drywall and coated sinkers and within minutes a pontoonboat arrived and I began the real work. I had no more to offer. The faded slogans chalked red on the cement wall reappear as the water rushes down the stairs. I need to go back for the hammer. Will the surf ingest me as a leukocyte might? I am a grit of irritation around which an iridescent sphere of calcium carbonate compound has formed. I have revealed my plumage to the mirror of my dressingtable with stoppered vials of pollen pheromone & perfume. Earthworms never get confused this way. I am decorating my nest with fruits flowers shells bones saliva dried grass charcoal and fruitpulp. At age 15 all men must participate in a ceremony in which they are the last person to be chosen for an athletic team. The fatal effect of social stress can cause death among those unfit to survive in rat colonies. How boxcars must feel when they have been left on unused track among dilapidated warehouses not certain for sure if ever an engine will be again by! A cigarettefilter can never be sure if it will be screwed out and extinguished in time in a dignified death or if the flame will char it in a scalding stench. The nocturnal prosimians, conversely, are a solitary species. Here is my vocabulary deprived of phonetics: it is up to you which words to emphasize. My early manuscripts were destroyed by Spanish invaders. My dialect retains traces of the people who colonized me: Arabic English French Portuguese Russian Spanish. As I write this letter the papyrus is aging beneath my engraving stylus and the middles are falling out of the Os in a white snow across the tabletop. I memorized this letter in signlanguage but sprained my wrist. I made this cool ginger drink. I can never send this letter. This much is clear. Bulldozers will demolish this letter. Its former inhabitants will return by sundown to build fires where the wreckage offers protection from the wind. The howling of the wolves will echo from a icosaphonic system with speakers fourteen stories tall. The constellations will follow the smooth tracking of the planetarium projector. For after this letter's internal logic has collapsed it is to be buffeted by fierce monsoons volcanoes and earthquakes for forty hours a week for forty weeks. It will be after the blackening of this letter's atmosphere allows the formation of glaciers which render its regions inhospitable to words. We'll be, after an immense comet collides with this letter, on an irregular orbit. Be afternoon or later probably. After all, what's in a letter? Letters. But what's in a letter? Phones or lines? It is me, stamped as though from cookie dough and arranged on the waxpaper you are holding now. Oh well. I love to hear the blues you two do. I'm glad its something you two can do. Due to the existing blues establishment in which the duet of Lamont and Tony is a deviation from the slick metallic polish of bigmoney hornsection late B.B.King or the continuing corruption perpetrated by white British guitarplayers whose colleagues all died in 1971 which is all an appropriation of acoustic music of genuine emotion. You two return me somewhere I've never yet been. After I listened to the song I listened to it again. And again. And a fuse blew and all my batteries went dead so I couldn't listen to anything else ever again. Although there's no beach at night one can stand atop small topographic circles and see a very distant horizon delineated by lights: farms autos trains electricity and industry all ornamenting the perimeter of a remarkably black sometimes blue sky carelessly scattered with constellations I hope I get a chance to rename with you, Lamont, under accessible userfriendly skies like this in which a shooting star is visible about once every seven seconds with the following exception: only one person can see it. By the time the rest have turned to look it never happened. It was just a joke. Listen I can try to make it up to you. I've got lots of shooting stars at home I can just mail you one. Do you have an address in the Florida sky? I urgently need to write you back. Your last correspondence came as quite a surprise to me. I had underestimated you yet again. However, in response, queen to rook 4. (Clue: this somewhat arcane tactic was renamed the Maledetto Gambit by its creator Anjali Gaburo.) Also, in our checkers match, in order, I hope, to live up to the impressive challenge you present, I will, as you may have guessed, make my only possible move. Finally, in what is now proving to be a fascinating Tic Tac Toe match, my next X will go in the lower right making it impossible for either of us to win. Lest I forget: in Monopoly I got doubles twice which landed me on Park Place and Boardwalk upon both of which I erected two hotels and as Banker I have already made the necessary transaction as well as adjusting the balance two hundred dollars for passing **Go** on my third roll, a 3 and a 4, which means I landed on, oh, some piece of property I don't think anybody owns. Hurry up and roll. Also: the interest on the small loan I granted you is due so please mail it with your next move, preferably in orderly hundreds. In response to your accusation that I have been embezzling from the

Bank: I am hurt. If I appear to have more money than I should it is merely because I am involved in two other simultaneous correspondence Monopoly games with one friend in Fargo and another in Mexico City. Both of these games are going very well for me and as a result I have a little extra Monopoly cash I have invested in our game. I reread the rules and as I suspected this type of strategy is not specifically forbidden anywhere. But Lamont, this is madness! Let us both put away the dice forever. I would rather we played a boardgame with no artificial money or simulated property, no tenements or luxury hotel casinos. They have thoughtmachines there. You put in a word and pull a lever and nothing happens. But sometimes bells ring lights blink and the machine writes you a poem, sometimes a novel of arbitrary length which can take quite awhile to reel out of the slot onto the floor. For awhile I thought it would stop. I thought I had written you every word I knew, but I discovered a word I forgot: Distended. Once I have found a sentence for the word Distended I will have my friends tape my mouth shut and tape bulky mittens over my hands and I will stand in the corner and nod occasionally. But what sentence? "My memories of you are distended with your unknown response to my more-than-10-page letter looming largest although invisible through which I can see the still-really-large most recent 6 page letter from you and cassettes somehow larger and more important than our foreshortened telephone conversations and distant January..." Nah. I can come up with a better sentence than that I'm sure. I don't know much, Lamont, and am not convinced that I am more likely to gain wisdom by articulating my opinion than by delighting in the predictably weird behavior of pelicans. I cannot take my eyes off of the sky outside. I sit helmeted at a table as other people's opinions ricochet around a classroom. "Shoot louder!" Herbert barks to a student with a silencer. I become unmuted slowly. Nevertheless, These ?The Paranoid and Guilt-Riddled Weeks? have still been some of the best weeks I've ever had, considering seventh grade. Did I speak up then? I only wanted to hide. I roamed the golfcourse at night. Seventh heaven, seventh hell. To get off I overdosed on candy purchased at 7-11. I was scarecrow and decoy, repellant and lure, aphrodisiac and steroid. I was the days of the week, Monday through Friday except holidays. On seventh thought the Spirit of the *Seventeen Seas* Magazine. Um... I wish I had raised my hand during practice of the Edison Middle School Varsity Band and asked: "Mr.Johnson, please don't throw your baton at me but I just wanted to ask: um, I've noticed during our intensive and, shall I say, eternal rehearsals of this piece of music colloquially entitled, um (shuffling of sheetmusic) "Oh When the Saints go Marchin' In" when I play the notes notated for my B^b clarinet here it sounds like the other instruments are playing different notes but it's hard to tell because the whattaya-call-it, um (shuffling of pages of Music Theory textbook brought from home) "timbres" are different and, I'm guessing, everyone is waythehelloutoftune. Are we supposed to play different notes? Also, what is "harmony?" Please don't whip your baton at me sir." But I didn't. I am more fortunate than most but much of my education is unaccounted for. I watch you flower ideas sown in the Tallahassee Florida soil and want to lie down beside you. Accept rain and fertilizer. They will point at my weeds and flash their shears. If I was a birch tree in autumn and you were sleeping beneath me in summer, I would lean with the wind to tickle your nose with my lowest twig. If you twitched murmured something rubbed your upperlip and continued to sleep, I might playfully drop an oval leaf on you. Thus emboldened I might let fall another. Another. Overwhelmed with giggles I might then vigorously shake myself bare so you would wake up buried to your nose in leaves and I would pose innocently bleached and skeletal against the winter sky. Eventually they would come calling for you. Lamont? Lamont! Speak to me! Are you alright? You fell off a ladder and hit your- Don't try to move! Just wait here I'll get you a cold drink... We've got lemonade and cider—cold or hot (which is really good with ginger, nutmeg, and a cinnamonstick)—and of course milk (2%) and coffee and tea, all kinds of coffee and tea actually, or water with or without ice... Say, did you know that hot water freezes faster than cold water? Is that because of water's unique property of expanding during crystallization? Also, hot water is lighter per volume than cold water. Is that because it's less dense? No no, lie back down, let me get you something to drink. Well, I guess you're right. If you aren't actually hurt, as you say, than it in fact does not, as you say, make any sense for you to lie down. I guess I hadn't thought of that. Right now I am starting a list of all the things I haven't thought of yet. I have done some strategic reorganizing of my brain. In order to avoid continually tripping over memories of you I have piled them all up against the back wall with a solid layer of thoughts fantasies and memories sealing them in. It's rumbling but I think it will settle down. Uh oh! It's bursting! Ideas concepts equations trivia and preconceptions are flying all over the place! Is it possible for me to have feelings for a woman which are romantic, sexual, or just goofy without being a rapist, gaybasher, or just trite? If so, tell me how at once. Because all evidence suggests that mostly heterosexual men of Western European descent screw up the world. Everyone else gets to use a banner as an umbrella. Until 1992 I was not comfortable being called a "man." I preferred "boy" or "guy" (coinage indicating adult boy). But in 1992 someone referred to me as "man" and I got used to it. It made me want to wear a tie make good eyecontact and have businesscards printed up which read

W a i t e r : W r i t e r : F r e a k

"...have bowtie & laptop, will travel..."

However, as a werdnerd, I do not feel that my needs are being met by the present society. I demand a better selection of technical magazines and 24hour reference rooms every block. I demand more illustrations, executed with care and exact measurements. In studying this letter, scientists now urge the use of compositional techniques as this extended improvisational semantic juggling act is exhausting. But did William even know Lamont well enough to open his skull and reveal to her the workings of his delusions? By now you understand my plan. To start writing this letter again every sentence with no sign of stopping, that's the sort of must-have-a-lot-of-spare-time-for-a-person-with-such-a-small-attention-span-kind-of-guy I am, kind of. I no longer feel the compulsion, inflicted upon me by a society intent on alienating people by coupling them, to mail these letters to you in expectation of a response or even at all. This is a major step for me. Once I showed Rick about sixteen or so pages and he merely responded by mentioning them in a carefully restrained burst of actual sentiment for me in marginalia in a letter to Laurel whose last name nobody knows. Nobody need know anything about this letter. Except the publishers of the future. And in 2001 when I'm a trendy novelist whose name appears in raised gold type on thick paperbacks sold in supermarketlines above the fascist crosswordpuzzle weightloss propaganda and splendid periodicals like an article in the *National Inquirer* which begins "Suzy's tubby hubby..." or an issue of *Time* with a story called "Evil—We're not sure what it is but it has nothing to with any of the companies that advertise in our periodical with bland clipped grammatically laughable sentences like:

> You need Shorter Sentences. Fewer of them.
> Fragments too. Because all those clauses can get in your way.
> And you've got a long way to go.
> And when you get to the top, you'll be able to look down.
> And that's Important.
> And that's why We're Us."

and in a tiny row along the bottom of the page are photographs of multinationalcorporateexecutives and their husbands. And then you hear a small voice saying "as an extremely trite person I am offended by the manner in which the present society has overused its clichés." As a person trying to become caring intelligent communicative organizational and constructive, I find that the present society is not making it easy. If I were paid to read our culture would benefit more than it does from my services as waiter. My knowledge would belong to everyone. I want to earn less, learn more. The experts on how to earn have employed me. Knowledge is all right there: at the 3rd Largest University Library System in America (or Something) which is about ten blocks away from my desk with only one busy street to cross. It is free but the system in which I earn hides the system in which I can learn. I turn this model of knowledge inside out and smear fistfuls of it across the paper for you but it will not last long. Suppose I learned the intricacies of the elaborate dances in which honeybees encode the location and type of flower? Society's response would be to send the military in on a peacekeeping mission to harvest the flowers to prevent the bees from terrorizing them, to carpetbomb the entire garden with deadly insecticides to protect our valuable nectar. I am unable to feed myself and the workers chew my food for me. We force the queens to fight. Why can't there be more than one queen? We are all flapping so hard. I have found nectar. Up down down. Snapdragons and marigolds. Left right right. There is a threat of wasps. Circle circle. We must defend the queen, at least until she finishes her novel. She is already on the first paragraph which reads "I remember the night the world ended. The incessant rain put out the powerplants and the flooding toppled dams and swept away cars. The women gathered together above the clouds on the pinnacles of coastal mountains. The tidal waves, mud, and landslides made them extremely treacherous. Lightning lashed and the rain flashed. We men, for the first time in 2000 years, huddled together for warmth in a chink in the stone, hoping the earthquakes would not return to crush us as they had the others. Many fled to the deserts in fear of further volcanic eruptions. A few tried to find the women. If any of them did, they never made it back. We didn't talk about the women out loud for fear one of us would use the old tongue and the skies would hear. We had a special handsignal that meant "women" and another that meant "a woman I knew before the end of the world." We spent most of the day in silence trying to remember everything we could." There came a knocking at the door. The queen looked up from her typewriter, annoyed. A

47

worker entered, buzzing designs for a better society. It will have to have espresso machines and grinders. Is this immoral? I hope so. Once we've abolished morality we can stop having wars. There is no order, moral or otherwise, that transcends the best interests of its people. Yet the system is more important than its elements. Our nation's economy is more important than our nation's people. We're here to serve the people. We opened this restaurant on behalf of its customers. I am not comfortable with my id in these awkward times. Somebody handed me a cup of punch. It turns out there was Lamont in it. Nobody told me. I've been up for three months. It's this Lamont. It just won't quit. I need something to bring me down and make me miserable again. I have an abnormal growth on my heart and, because I am not sure if it is benign or malignant, I don't want to have it looked at. By anyone. I'm sorry I mentioned it. It had been fifteen days since our last phone conversation and I was a quaking wreck when you at last called. I want a free plastic frog. Most men my age do but won't admit it. Hello up there. I'm the tiny man who lives in your desk drawer the landlady was telling you about. I've solved all your problems. I put your in basket in your out basket and got rid of it which means no more paperwork for you. I did the same thing with your rolodex and phone so now you have no choice but to compose music using company paper and pencil and eraser (I think we have staff staffpaper in one of the cabinets in the basement) or to compose writing using the IBM Wheelwriter 9 that we've supplied—extra ribbons on the top shelf just buzz me if you need anything. I'll be in your desk drawer composing sculpture with company paperclips. Who am I kidding? You remember my squished up face, but are you aware that you are receiving letters from a man 616 feet and 8 inches tall? I believe that if I stood on my own shoulders I could scale the Sears Tower. The Sears Tower would notice me, unlike the columns of tiny businesspeople and sightseers who all day trickle imperceptibly through its entrails, ride its effortless elevators. For the first time the Sears Tower might believe that people did build it, its mammoth rectilinear majesty 101 feet taller than the World Trade Center not including the additional 579 feet above sealevel. Here is a man who can look it in the window even when I stand up to my knee in Lake Michigan. I can see it from here it looks close enough to touch. I am typing using a microscope and a pool cue. It is worse than threading a needle. I can't read the screen at all. Frustrated I stamp my computer into a glowing smear of electronic firefly paste. I am going to jog to your house in one afternoon. I will crash through the Ohio River leaving footprints into whose depths whirlpools spiral. The river will finally get a playmate sufficiently bigger than a fish. It will encircle my waist like a playful serpent. It will rain down from my soaked Tshirt splattering craters, rendering the floodplains marshland. I try not to snap trees but some of them are very small. I blow the rainclouds away. What if I step on a deer by accident? What if I step on Atlanta? What if I step on an overpass over a busy highway? I leap over Pensacola blotting radar and plunge into the Gulf. What will I say to you? Will my voice crack concrete for miles around? Will my voice be detectable to the human ear? What use will I be to you when Florida crumbles into the Atlantic? Seagulls and pelicans are landing in my hair, fighting over the herring entangled there. I can lurk in Tampa Bay submerged to my eyes until I see you. Then I will blow bubbles. If I can grow to the size of a mountain can I shrink to the size of a molehill, no bigger than a breadbox? I will crawl up the clifflike concrete steps and through the grass toward the looming Rita Kip Music Room where you are teaching your operaclass. I am startled by a ladybug which falls from a tall blade of grass onto my back, knocking me over. It waves its glistening antennae ambivalently and jerkily ascends another blade. I duck behind a dandelion as students walk by talking about Jonathan Swift. I stub my toe on a penny from 1926. Finally I am inside crawling along the baseboard toward your backpack. I hope I don't meet any more ants. Some of them are faster than me. I crawl through the zipper and try to find a place in the binding of a threering where I won't get crushed when you pick me up. With a piece of pencil lead I begin to write out what I will say to you when I reenlarge in your living room and you see your backpack explode to reveal me, zipper in my hair, canvas scraps around my shoulder, standing grinning in the radius of pencils thrown from the blast. Whatever I say right then better be good. Hi. Do you remember the flavors of my breath? Could you tell I was a safely unstable man? My 8 incisors the must of nicotine. My 4 canines blackened from many a caffectomy. Did my 8 premolars (bicuspids) taste like residue of rancid cocaine from 1991 when I failed to get off for the third time? Did the flavor clash with my 12 molars—the strychnine tinge of the bad acid? My younger lover: near my impacted wisdom tooth did your tongue find the musk of marijuana? My mouth is not a temple; it is a scuffed dormroom with tapemarks where the Rolling Stones posters were torn down. Will my teeth always be covered by gelatinous plaque? I am afraid that excessive acid may have fractured my ectodermal enamel. Decay may be imminent. I ingested corrosive sugar and carbohydrates in the fantasy that my teeth were deciduous. Despite rigorous orthodonture a failure to wear my retainer on many a moonlit teenage night may have resulted in poor alignment. Do I have all 32? I am afraid to count. Why didn't I protect my crown and the root from the neck down? Have I damaged my delicate mesodermal pulp of capillaries, nerves, lymphatics? I fear I may have weakened the cementum in which my porous dentine roots are buried. I knew not what I was eating. Do you remember the articulations of my fingertips? Could you tell I was a dangerously stable man? In my caresses did you feel echoes of the cats and women I have touched? Did my 14 phalanges retrace the contours of Johann Sebastian Bach, a coffeepoint Siamese whose affection arose from a scientist's intellect and genuine love for all living things especially birds. Did I scratch you behind the ears? Sorry if I did. My 5 metacarpals were taught to love Wolfgang Amadeus Mozart who would curl like a conch in my lap radiating purrs in a loud and shameless bliss. My 8 carpal bones explored your humerus sacrum and articular processes erasing the older tapes. Was my trapezium hesitant? It remembered the one who would punish me through electrodes wired to my low self esteem centers. Sextortion. When it became clear that she considered me her property I began to vandalize myself. My trapezoid did not want to confuse you with the two women with whom I shared sex without intimacy. My scaphoid: confused groping with a stranger. Embarrassing sex? Worse, my lunate, boring sex. My pisiform had not recovered from its first kiss, recoiling from eellike tongue. Only my hamate had a clue to you. There was another Lamont once. She kissed me to life then lay me to rest, and my libido has dozed fitfully since. I believed that if I memorized you I could recreate you in Illinois, my capitate painting you into existence in the basement air. And what about my triangular? I'm not sure when my mother stopped touching me except for obligatory hugs but it must have been sometime after my father stopped touching me including obligatory hugs. Hi. I'll have to knock down walls to fit these characters into the letter I'm writing. The latter is litter, an assortment of any old joke I dragged in off the street. The former are my psychic toy figurines I set up every year or so. I want to knock down some walls, they have channeled my thoughts into a maze of relevancies that will never touch paper. I, again I, then me, myself. I have been reduced to a conduit, once a battery, I know not where the electrons flow. Thought through me to anyone who needs it at the speed of discourse as synaptic relays click. A vicious recoil from the personality I had assumed to meet with deal with people not altogether perfectly into the nondimensional linearity of my solitude, the disintegration of my muchpolished individuality. I failed, I succeeded. Nihilistic inefficiencies multiply, spent and squandered eclipsed here. And I try to believe what I admit to be true. So the butterfly wanders away while I, framed in a picture window, ruminate the methods of linguistic literary antiquity: so many avenues of dissatisfaction open why does one roar with the vacuum of inevitability, a waterfall..? why no composition why only improvisation why no why no? whine, oh wino. no. Why these sentences they are more channels of cut stone my thoughts rush down irrigating? Now there are only lights from a few scattered campfires. Why i me, why can't this voice roam through language free and unattached to questionmarks periods and capitaletters even beginnings and endings? Observe the architectures of the neighborhoods in which we upgrew. See how the rooms tend to separate people but prevent activity? See how two adjacent houses never share a lawn a bench or picnictable? Is every family a sentence? Is every home a prison? Suddenly you wake up at your desk where you had fallen asleep in your textbook reading the following passage:

Chapter Question:
-What is the unique evolutionary advantage of the telephone?-

Four billion years ago conditions on earth were unsuitable for inventions. The atmosphere consisted of hydrogen, methane, ammonia, and watervapor. There were no grounded outlets and the sky was wracked with powersurges. From these corrosive beginnings crude unicellular phones were created spontaneously. Within a million years the phone had adapted to life on shore and telephone poles towered above the earth. Various adaptations have made the phone better able to compete with other inventions: the Strowger Electromechanical Selector, the answering machine, the beeper. Scientists believe these adaptations came about in response to hostile conditions through random mutation. However, the remains of a fossilized phone unearthed in Scotland by Alexander Graham Bell resembles a footprint found by Elisha Gray near Chicago dated to about the same era. Are telephones indigenous to North America or did they migrate across a giant land bridge stretching across the Atlantic from Eastern Siberia to Tierra Del Fuego? In examination of the structure of those primitive inventions believed to be predecessors to the phone—the telegraph, lightning, the wheel—it becomes tempting to ascribe the genesis of the phone to a divine creator. Similarly, when one looks at descendants of the phone—the cordless phone, cable television, the Fender Stratocaster—the telephone itself begins to appear a bit simple. And most *individual* phones are quite simple. It is the existence of an electrical network connecting all phones— Mickey Mouse phones, easily broken $10 phones, ostentatious antique phones (usually found in bars with "character")—that is the unique property of the phone which makes it more sophisticated than, say, the compact disc player. Phone linkups are used by computers to transmit information around the world at an extremely high rate. The ability of the phone to relay information surpasses that of people. Or does it? Many have taken a more holistic approach. Human society and the telephone are interdependent, so why separate them into two different phenomena with their own histories? As Gillespie pointed out (1993) "the telephone is an evolutionary adaptation more significant than air breathing lungs, analogous to the opposable thumb. The telephone is remarkable in a way that the lung, hand, and mind is not. Rather than make each individual better able to survive, the telephone makes the human species better able to survive. For the advantage of the phone lies in its potential to help humans coordinate their needs on a larger scale. The telephone network has finally made it possible to think of the human species as a single entity. The next step is the ability to coordinate the needs of the human species with those of all the other species. This is the true progress of evolution: back to a single unicellular organism." Maybe so. Yet... Everyone talks about the Bang as if it were a great party that got a little out of control. I remember the time before. What I remember is that I was not me, I was all matter and so was everybody else and the burning unity, the singularly hot and dense intimacy, was a far better universe to me than the slow astronomical ballet we are playing out now, stretched for millennia as imperceptibly thinning dust. You are about to give me advice: maybe I should join a star. I assure you, it is not the same. Being a star seems nice and warm, really bright and industrious, until you grow cold and collapse. Then when the gravity is so strong not even light can escape, the other particles start to get really irritating. Before the Bang: that was different. That was before I was an electron. As soon as someone decided they were a separate particle and tried to leave everything just blew up and now there is time: awful dull slow time. During the expansion I did what every electron did. I got a hydrogen molecule together in the hopes that we would someday undergo fusion and become a heavier, more stable molecule. We tried to bond with other particles but strangely I find myself continually repelled by other electrons. We drifted for awhile and got a gig in a dust cloud orbiting itself. We picked up enough matter that we collapsed and formed a solar system. Yeah, every electron's dream, I know, but it took forever. We just kept on accelerating and accelerating but it never felt like we were moving. I was lucky enough to get involved in a planet and we lived it up. I was heavily into methane and was in more than one lightningbolt. Then one night a bunch of us formed unicellular lifeforms. We didn't know what we were doing. About this time I really started wishing I could get off the planet. No luck. I spent a lot of time in plants and animals which were getting larger and more complex every millennia. It wasn't that great. At least in the unicellular lifeforms everyone knew each other. We'd be plankton, get absorbed by a whale, beach, be assimilated by carrion, then a bug, then some bird would ingest us and so on. I was even involved with a—you guessed it—human. Wait, here's the ironic part. This human was selected somehow by its species, I'll never understand why, for a special project. They put it in a special container and shot it into space. Now I sit by a tiny round window watching my planet, my host, my body, pirouette slowly across a gulf of emptiness as I write my memoirs. I am nostalgic for that time before the Bang. I look at the other electrons in my molecule (I am in Oxygen now. I know. Thanks.) whom I will never meet. And I look at the other molecules in my cell. I look at the other cells in my body and down below or up above are the other bodies in my species, the other species in my ecosystem, the other ecosystems on my planet, the other planets, the other planetary systems... See? I long for a time when there was no plurality, only a singularity. Maybe it will happen again someday. Maybe this is only the beginning. Maybe my molecule and I will take on larger and larger projects. We have had a few really long periods of work. Silly molecule. Now you are a human. You didn't know what you were getting into. How you long to drift through the void again. It will join the atmosphere, it will be the atmosphere. Not a freefloating particle among freefloating particles but somehow the entire atmosphere. It encircles the earth filtering radiation absorbing heat selfcleaning and cooling in storms and currents. Grounding its own collected electrons. It will be the ocean whose vapor permeates it. It will be the species that inhale and exhale it, that absorb and excrete the water. It will be the radiation of the sun that is accepted screened reflected by it, photosynthesized and absorbed by it. It will be the phases of the moon, the eclipses, the tides, but the stars will remain constellations. The void is a spherical window it can never return beyond. It is earth and it is everything it needs. It will find a way. Humans will evolve by becoming Humanity whose survival is the shared purpose of each, the way I was before the Bang, before matter was scattered in particles. Humans will become Earth. Earth will become Universe. I am nostalgic for the days before the separation. Following the first ice age came a century of floods and phones adapted to high rocky places to avoid being shorted out. There were many predators. Telephone poles were often knocked down by mammoth automobiles. Early ships were so big they could support their own weight only when partially submerged. Gradually steam engines were replaced by gasoline engines: an adaptation making cars better suited to life on land. Interestingly, while the motorcycle is a member of the same phylum as the automobile, the bicycle is not. The bicycle is related to the sailboat and the glider: ecologically sustainable transportation. The bicycle is in fact the natural enemy of the automobile which will charge on sight. All appliances reproduce asexually through mass production (see Chapter 6: Capitalism). Given the improbability that an appliance so intricate could have evolved by chance, it is tempting to ascribe the genesis of the paperclip to a creator. Geneticists are struggling to create the videophone—a hybrid television. Even the television shows a failure to adapt: lousy audio fidelity when compared to today's compact disc player which usually has a skip button instead of a numberpad much the way certain digital clock alarms can be set backwards five minutes only by advancing forwards 1435 minutes. But even this seems more sophisticated than the telephone's dial. Call me Lamont I am King of the House the others have politely left me to my reign. I sleep on the modular sofa beside a pile of books. I type at the dining room table drinking coffee without guilt. I will arc like a bullet on a trajectory. I will have a direction and speed like a vector and I will circumnavigate the globe in my shoes. I will eat a large breakfast and return to bed triumphant. Somehow I will drag my ass through the next three workdays and anything left over is mine to keep. I don't want to so much look good as be good, because Lamont's coming. And I will make of myself a gift for her. Ever will there be a finer motivation? Can I stuff my gut back full of my scattered entrails and prop myself up on my doorstep? Just as I had hired a team of female and male scientists from around the world to help produce state of the art letters for you, the night you arrived my house with bustling with restaurateurs hired from a broad spectrum of ethnic fullservice restaurants. To provide a menu unavailable elsewhere we cooked entirely using endangered species. We try to offer a few extinct specials each day. This week we have some Dodo—frozen of course—and the bald eagle paté is always excellent. When you arrived a host greeted you and offered to take your coats. I had no time to maintain my health and hygiene in my rush to prepare the final separation of mind & body. I know quitting cigarettes is easy: I've done it at least twice this year alone. Did you put your ear to my brittle ribcage and hear my breath roar rasping? Splinter my motives shaven and calm. For a month you will see me come and go, taut in the morning and slack in evening I will run past your house twice a day, jogging to Florida and back. My limbs whistling crabs ticklish and underwater lounging in the fluorescent depths they spurt ink in clouds... It was a mouth stuffed with syllables which did not know you were coming. I drink smart drinks now: fluoridated orange juice with extra vitamin X. I have fissure sealing: A groove deepened with a drill and filled with molten plastic. What would I be doing right now if not writing? I will dance this rigid two step alone, but not for too much longer. I can no longer write anything except letters to Lamont. I tried so hard to shake it. It wouldn't come unstuck.

Shaker broken in the game. I wanted off the riverboat then. Institutional gambling facility or no I wanted to plunge into the icy grey. I got sad when I couldn't not write letters to you. I wanted to write nonsense, pornography, heavy metal lyrics, bad checks, postcards to Patch Adams—my professional doctor and clown friend. My motives dissolved as my musculature molten in a sea of lactic acid. that mono nucleosis feeling. I am a base and sensual man, but have fewer friends, kisser without kissees. Especially now. Jean le Necre is dead. I found him today upon returning from a feed store with 10 pounds of fresh cedarshavings and .5 pounds of sunflowerseeds. He and I were going to spend our first afternoon together in months and I was going to let him be warmed by sunlight, cooled by breezes, overwhelmed by grass twice his height filled with weird stuff to eat and be eaten by. I was going to, for the first time since winter, remove him from the tomb of basement in which we were living and let him scramble through the yard. There he lay. A limp arc of black. Sleek, gerblesque, triped. I buried him beneath a wooden block and spread the old cedar sunflower husks across the earth. I never had a chance to explain irony to him but I think somehow he understood. He would never see the naked sunlight in 1993 crawling with life. He would never understand that for all his isolation alone in a dry aquarium he was one facet of a extensive and complex family of various species all intertwined interrelated and interdependent. An embarrassing family album he never chewed, in solitude in a test tube. Since the demise of his brother Rotary Torsion Wrench. I could have been a better father to him I admit. How many emotional breakdowns and personality revisions of mine had he witnessed? He was a mouse crawling through the dust wires and pipes behind the continually repainted cardboard of my facade. If only I could hold him in my hand and offer him a dandelion — something he could only eat, never understand. Now I feel alone. No more pets. Somewhere in the house Rick plays a weird chord on guitar and I wince in solitude. These walls seem like a prison now. And now I am walking the plank above a weekend filled with sharks. These are the remarks that the hecklers in my head jeer. I want to write them on the wall in red chalk. When they say "I" I do not know who they are talking about. I share the weapons of my own self-inflictions with you, what I use to prevent old wounds from healing. What I use to hurt myself, masking the pain of others, thereby taking control of my own suffering:

> I hate myself hate myself I want to kill myself
> Kill me I am hated Ignore me I wish I had never
> been born I love agony Who cares I hate hate
> I want me I am me I wish I love Who?

Who invited them to the funeral? Jean le Necre? Jean le Necre? Did you die of neglect the day I stopped neglecting you? The day I had an automobile and ten bucks to throw on a cornucopia of organic luxuries for you my friend? Poet grieved by the departure of a rodent. I hardly knew ye. How could I? Still struggling to cope with the ropes of my own existence. You lived with me in eight places in the past three years, only three of which were basements, only two of which were my parents. You had peripheral relations with many a freak of the human species, my friends, and were terrorized by rock music as well as Bach and Mozart. My last pet has been torn from me by our different metabolisms and cruel incessant time. Time time time, see what's become of me. Time is flowing like a river. Time is waiting in the wings, she speaks of senseless things, her script is you and me. Time takes a cigarette, puts it in your mouth. I've got too much time on my hands. Time keeps on slipping slipping slipping into the future. The time is gone the song is over. I need a new metaphor for time. Time is not running out, nor is it money, nor does a stitch in it save nine. Time flies are crawling in my eyes. Time flies when you're having fun, and I'm having none. Time is not the orbits of a clock nor the orbits of earth sun and moon nor the sand in an hourglass. I am always afraid I won't have enough time to do everything I want to do. To solve this dilemma I can either A. want to do fewer things or B. alter my conceptualization of time so that there is always enough. I have seen the machinery of time screw a gerbil into the ground.

I can already feel the pressure twisting me deeper. Lamont, help. Did you know that you rescue me? You hear my voice echoing up from the thick blue deep. Did you know I was lonely? My bubbles erupt on the surface. Are you going to sprinkle the food? I can see your silhouette flattened in the silvery plane of air above. You know I would overeat, but will you overfeed me? I hear the shrill pitch of your whistle and feel the others leave the pool. Will you splash through the surface and swim down to me to drag me to the sun, to resuscitate me with kisses? Within the barnacleencrusted planks of my ancient hull, I am convinced, tarnished doubloons glint partially buried in liquid sand. Do you know about my pearl? I can't wait until you. You will bring me to the surface before permanent braindamage results from hypoxemia. I have reason to gulp the air coughing choking seawater. My soaked lungs on the verge of collapse, angling rib punctures pneumothoracic cavity. Will you emerge from bobbing in the basin soaked and triumphant with apple me in your teeth? I am the duck with the lucky number as you swing your magnet in on the end of the pole...Will we click? I cram for the exam. No longer underwater, no longer undergraduate. I break the surface with three days and two nights transfer credit at the Summer School for Designing Lamont and William. The Summer School for Lamont and William is a ten day session during which two people will study one another intensively. The roles of teacher and student will be switched often, as will the roles of cook waiter and customer. During a "problem jostle" (a term used by cyberneticians) within the first two days the curriculum will be decided by both participants. Possible courses for July 1993 include:

Breakfast 101—Introduction to Breakfast.
coffee
Snack 202.
bread
Dinner 103—Special Courses.
     Section A. asparagus-artichoke soup
     Section B. olive-feta salad
Dinner 304—The Entrée: 1700 to the Present.
almond-ginger
Dessert 106—Eastern European Pastries.
baklava
Dessert 107—Evolutionary Perspectives.
coffee

Grounds of the school consist of a house which consists of a kitchen, a listening room, a library, a collage crayon and lego room, and a lavish yard. Within walking distance of the school is a magical forest that nobody else knows about populated by deer elves and the two student bodies of the Summer School for Lamont and William. Students are encouraged to start a band, to take long walks together, and to talk about stuff. However, if I were one of your friends hearing you tell of your plan to drive to an extremely flat state to meet an extremely narrow guy I would try to talk you out of coming here to see me. Why? As your friend I would be jealous of your desire to spend time with me, rather than with me. By this logic I have become jealous of myself. What do I have that I don't have? I don't know what she sees in me. It's not fair. If I only had the qualities that I have... I tried to get her to notice me but she only has eyes for me. Sigh. I wish I were me. Some guys have all the luck. This is the first time I've written a letter long enough that Rumplestiltskin could climb it to my tower window. That's right: I'm Rapunzel again. And, like many classical Western romantic heroines, I am trapped in a tower waiting for my classical Western romantic hero. Do you know Lancelot? I can only hum a few bars. Do you speak any

Romeo? You could play Menelaus. Man, ever do Don Juan and Don Quixote de la Mancha at the same time? Wild. This letter was written for you by Cyrano de Bergerac, who is far too far in love with me to risk admitting it. I guess that makes me Guinevere, Juliet, Helen, 700 mistresses in Italy 800 mistresses in Germany 91 in Turkey and France and in Spain 1003, Dulcinea, and Roxanne. As long as I don't have to read all that crap I'll be any combination of archetypical helpless females you select. I'm ready. Why am I attracted to you in this way? Is it gravitational? Electromagnetic? If this is the weak force I wonder what the strong force feels like... Bang! At that moment the door slammed: my housemate Andy had arrived home from Waxahachie, Texas where he flew to look at the supercolliding superconductor, I mean superconducting supercollider. I guess that's kind of like Disneyland for physics majors. Except it isn't built yet. Like Epcot if, that is, Epcot were an unbuilt unfunded dream which would remain under construction for all eternity. I remember when I was just a blueprint inscribed in combinations of proteins. I might never have been built. I might not have met you like I didn't when Lightning Sam Hopkins and my band opened for you at Fillmore in 1968. There were dozens of teenage boys carrying steaming casserole dishes to your dressing room. Backstage I saw you rasping rapping with a roadie but I was too cool to check you out. Way cool. That reminds me: it's refrigerator mating season, which accounts for the strange chirping our whirlpool emits. It's getting to me. Our neighbor left their screendoor unlatched. Their refrigerator escaped and now it is standing in our backyard, outside our kitchen window, chirping to our Whirlpool. Our unpaid electrical bill is making me think about Tony's friend's money. Remember the night we danced? Remember the money who drove into Tallahassee in the middle of the night we danced in the wallet of Tony's friend in a red convertible which ran on pure Kuwaiti oil? Just off the plane from London where he had gone (without telling his parents) to attend several art auctions. He had a few paintings in trunk by Rembrandt and Mondrian indicating he was a man of either eclectic taste or none at all. He drove a beautiful sharklike ultramasculine rented convertible and drank a terrible swilllike ultramasculine purchased Bud Light. Sideburns and expensive folio books. His cool haircut was an evolutionary adaptation: somewhere between hair all over the body and no hair whatsoever, slightly more advanced than me. When he opened his wallet to pay for the ice cream a geyser of money erupted whirling a cyclone up into the black sky. He spoke little as cool sexuality had given him laryngitis. I was so fascinated by his money, even as I handed him the Luigi Nono tape to crank on the pristine quadraphonic convertible sound system built for testosterone surge distortion of a L.L.Cool J.Zeppelin ilk. Where did the money come from? When I was money I was in his wallet for months and it kept on getting more crowded. Like a can of rabbits. When he finally spent me on gasoline (there were smaller bills but I was the first one he grabbed) I ended back up in his wallet a week later after an unmemorable tour of the banking system. Anyway I'd rather be an American dollar than an American any day. More respect. I am a twenty and I bear the face of Andrew Jackson, the president whose Indian Removal Policy caused every Native American east of the Mississippi to lose their home. Deflation has made the aging process more degrading, but I still make fun of singles. Washington: Ha! With an America so tiny, there was a limit to how cruel any administration could be. Jackson: there was a true bastard, arguably crueler than Reagan/Bush. The economy has "self-regulating mechanisms" which prevents it from responding to the interests of the people it controls, the people it supposedly functions to serve. We've got to get this nation's economy back on its feet, back on our toes. Then I can finally get a job in a restaurant, this time as a table. The customers come and go, speaking of DaVinci, leaving butts in my ashtray and gum stuck underneath me, eating Humpback Whale appetizers, Hairy-Nosed Wombat and Orangutan gumbo, and entrees of fresh Seal sauté. I could be a dish in a recursive restaurant. I think that's where, say, if you look at the menu and order chicken, then you are taken to another restaurant inside the first one where you look at the menu and decide how you want your chicken cooked, then you are taken to another restaurant inside the second restaurant where you look at the menu and decide how you want your grilled chicken seasoned...That can get expensive, paying all those bills at the end. I don't think you ever get your food. But what could I, as a table, offer you, as a philosopher, juggler, musician, acrobat, scientist, tapdancer, engineer, storyteller, architect... You could fill every available hole with pigeons and still have birds left over to offer to the sky. I too remember being a cow cursed by intelligence. I would stand there too, too indignant to graze, watching all those stupid bovines chewing their collective cud with profound complacency. I was a cow with frown lines who dreamed of kicking down the fence. I wanted to learn to speak in pitch timbre volume, hue chroma value, meter rhyme image, line shape texture: sound color words and pictures. I swore then that if I was ever a worm on a hook underwater and you were a hungry rainbow trout, I would stall you with the following riddle:

What am I?

I am just the way things are.

All human interactions involve both loss and gain.

I am responsible for the distribution of necessities—-which is funny, because their distribution doesn't interest me.

What interests me? Their possession.

Let me explain: within me, all nonabstract nouns can be subcategorized under possessive proper nouns. Verbs cannot possess nouns. Ownership is not based on usage.

It is not enough to be—one must do.

I impose symmetry on the asymmetrical: generosity becomes manipulation, gifts become bribes, requests owe favors.

Time can be measured therefore sold.

Because of me, you are lucky to have a job.

If I could convince animals and plants that it was in their best interests to work for me I would. Instead I sell them.

I am just the way things are:

This sentiment does not reflect, it projects.

What am I?

More urgently, how can I express the extent of my foolishness with a mere 26 letters predictably capitalized and punctuation? Well? Give up yet? The next paragraph is **3-D** and you will need special glasses to read it! But wait that's not all! Be careful when you turn the page because this is a ***Pop-Up letter***! That's right there are paragraphs in different planes but that's not all! This next sentence has scratch'n'sniff nouns. Be careful—this letter has real stainedglass panels. Every fabulous letter of this fabulous letter can be yours! As soon as it is finished. Meanwhile you are two weeks away. I need to finish this letter by then so as you walk in the front door I can hand it to you and collapse from exhaustion and sleep for 112 hours. Otherwise, after I have met you as a person, I'm sure it will be difficult to fantasize about you in this fashion. Particularly as you will be standing reading over my shoulder as I type, bored and wanting to play. Lamont, wait. Before you meet me in person I think you should know the five most embarrassing things I am most embarrassed about while you still have time to reconsider.

1.   I live in Urbana Illinois.

2.   I work in a restaurant.

3.   I live in a basement.

4.   Adam Wisnewski is one of my closest friends

5.   I am a woody herbaceous dioecius annual which will grow in almost any climate. I often reach heights from 12 to 20 feet in a single growing season. My flowering top relieves the symptoms of asthma, glaucoma, chemotherapy, depression, boredom and writer's block. My fiber strands can be woven into durable rope, textiles, and canvas. I have been used for rigging and sails on many a sailing vessel from the fifth century BC through modern times (including "Old Ironsides," U.S.S. Constitution).

The oil of my seeds can be used to manufacture paints, fuel, paper (including the first drafts of the *Declaration of Independence*) and food. They have the highest concentration of essential fatty acids in the animal kingdom and only soybeans contain a higher concentration of protein. Because of my versatility, American farmers were once encouraged to grow me with the same Government sponsored extortion which today encourages the use of toxic pesticides manufactured by powerful American chemical corporations with skilled American lobbyists. It was illegal to not grow me in Virginia between 1763 and 1767. Back when you were Thomas Jefferson you grew me on your plantation, oh yes, and walked among my flowering buds in the Appalachian sunsets. Where did you get my seeds Tom? Is it true that you spent time on the streets of Paris? Did you score some Chinese eggs in a Turkish hashish parlor? Did it improve your waltzing? You are too old to know, I know, but did Tocqueville toke? In your farm journal on 16 March 1791 you compared me to tobacco. You wrote that I was of first necessity to the commerce and marine, in other words to the wealth and protection of the country. But tobacco? "...never useful and sometimes pernicious.... America imports William and will continue to do so." With a flourish I closed my journal and set my quill aside. I rang for a slave to bring more Dutch East India tea. Nobody came. The trouble with slaves is that they keep breaking and need to be replaced. It was the evening you were due from Florida where you had begun early negotiations. I did not know when your carriage would arrive and was quite nervous. I kept glancing at my hourglass. Every time a twig snapped within a furlong of Monticello I would leap to the door the words "Hi Lamont I am amphibious er I mean I am aphasic er rather I am asphyxiated with delight!" forming on my palate. What if your bus was delayed? As I jot this postcard I am waiting for you for hours for fun in a dreary greyhound station gazing a lazy glazed glare at the peanuts in the vending machine as aluminum flanked busses arrive and depart, arrive, and depart, arrive, and, depart. Where are you? What if you boarded the train they call The City of New Orleans by mistake? What if you had boarded a plane to Somalia by grave grave mistake and had the aisle seat beside a talkative UN peacekeeping missionary en route to exploit rich deposits of iron ore and gypsum? What if your ship was devoured by hurricanes in the Bermuda Triangle? What if you exploded on the launching pad? What if your handlebars came off? You know how I worry. What if your Mazda 323 had broken down on the Indianapolis beltway and your copilot and navigator Tony was pushing swearing and sweating uphill a ramp while you sat behind the wheel singing along with your Bessie Smith tape, as semis swerved around you on only eight wheels horns blaring? As Thomas Jefferson I had only envisioned a continental network of dirt roads with stone arch bridges on evenings like these, waiting for you. Black curls of oily smoke rose from the tallow candle. Shadows played on the curtains. I knew you would appear incarnate. The avatar of Lamont summoned by this prolonged incantation, my dance in the pentagram, flickering candles at the vertices. The night thickens and jagged lightning saws the sky. Tornado sirens begin. The ship is tossed and as my hammock lurches violently from side to side, I have nauseous dreams of meeting Lamont in the form of a mermaid. In these dreams I resent being in the form of a mermaid. I am wet and infuriated. I have a preconceived notion of the comments the tunafishermen will make and I am determined to remain mythical. Lamont Lamont come in Lamont. Blink and wait for the radar to take another sweep. Unload your torpedo tubes. Begin surfacing maneuvers. Up periscope. I am the blip reported by sailors for centuries. I am breathing through a straw. I see your duckbill break the surface before you waddle onshore on four webbed feet. I watch the moonlight flow as luminescent oil across the still pond. The muscles in your flank ripple currents as you lift a hoof and place it carefully. You were laying your eggs in the warm mud at the bottom. You paddled across the surface raising a thin wake of moonlight. Your shell disappeared into the ink. I knew if I stepped on a twig you would lift your nose and crash off into the underbrush, your white tail disappearing in birches. Would you come back? You had a twoway ticket. I watched the arrival times scroll by overhead. A plane was landing every thirty

67

seconds. Children fretted amid luggage and uncomfortable chairs. Parents reluctantly purchased hot dogs. Ice cream vendors and balloon salesmen wandered through the gate. Suddenly you emerged from the crowd. "C'mon," you grabbed my arm and explained "this is my favorite ride." I followed your eager laughter through the throngs of tourists looking for a place to throw my cotton candy. I was afraid of rides because I had never been on one because I was afraid of them, all of which seemed to me like a reasonable reaction to an expensive contrived neardeathexperience with machinery. The ride whose serpentine line we arrived at the end of us was called ProjectMercury. The KennedyAdministration sealed you inside the nosecone of an enormous rocket which was then, after a interminably long countdown filled with malfunctions and delays, blasted into the ionosphere in a parabolic arc to splashland somewhere in the SouthAtlantic where a helicopter would recover you. The line was really long and with the launches spaced months apart with one per capsule it looked like we would be in the July sun quite awhile clutching our huge reels of milliondollartickets. This ride had an aspect which I found terrifying. What if the helicopter never came? I lay in the stench of napalm and flies. The machine gun fire and distant screaming was an album side which would end. I stared at the canopy of jungle and smoke listening to the production values, trying to isolate the sound of the helicopter, trying to isolate the sound of the planes dropping fire. I strained to hear the jet. "there it is man listen this was recorded using the RollingStonesMobileStudio and some plane must have flown right overhead while they were recording this song but they kept the take man and you have to listen to the song like about a zillion times before you can hear the jet but its there hey didja ever listen to StairwaytoHeaven backwards?" I looked up at you and sensed you didn't like LedZeppelin as much as me. I glanced bashfully down at the Superhype albumcovers and Swansong recordlabels strewn in a mess across the recroom carpet, including my scratched and unplayable but groovy vintage pressing of *LedZeppelinIII* whose runoffgroove bears the meaningless but heavy quip from Alastair Crowley. I lifted the needle from the theramin solo in "WholeLottaLove." There was an uncomfortable silence which crescendoed as our breathing rates accelerated, then I sighed. I had been about to explain how Jimmy Page had, without a breath of credit, stolen the song "Dazed and Confused" from an American folksinger named Jake Holmes whose 1967 version of the song had come out while Zeppelin was still the Yardbirds with Jeff Beck and how cool that was and then go on to list the American bluesman who had been plagiarized in each song in each LedZeppelin album, but... you were absently humming *The Rite of Spring* while reading the liner notes of Ligeti's *Aventures*. I viewed your naked blazing emotions as if through a sheet of ice. For the first time it occurred to me that you might not even care about Brian Jones, whom I had intentionally set aside the next three days to explain to you and reveal my warped pressing of *Their Satanic Majesties Request* with the hologram. For the first time it occurred to me that I didn't need a nonstop power hit marathon brought to you by New Diet Crystal Cherry Pepsi Free Classic and New Miller Dark Light Dry Bock Special Reserve Limited owned by the same parent company as New Marlboro Medium Slim Light 120 Filter Menthol Extrawide. We Don't Need Another Guitar Hero by Tina Turner and before that I played a cut by the Kinks off their new compact disc. Great new CD out by them on the same record label who just released the Complete the Who Discography Box Set on sale now. I don't need Classic Rock Light because Lamont/William could be Jagger/Richards, even Lennon/McCartney. Couldn't we? Couldn't you and I accumulate a notebook full of songs if we spent long evenings in Hamburg at a piano? Until the Weimar republic is threatened by the rise of National Socialism. Then, of course, the curtain will close on *Der Silbersee* and as soon as party newspapers denounce you as a "Jew" I will flee with my family to Prague. There is not enough time to write songs. We must print and distribute the leaflets of the resistance. We must sleep as little as possible and conspire in whispers at secret basement meetings under yellow bulbs, even if we would rather flutter around them chasing one another in elliptical orbits which sweep out equal areas in equal time. Which you were not given at the Board Meetings, by virtue of your womanhood. The last day I ever saw you, long before I became VP, I remember when we took our seats around the conferencetable in the conferenceroom where we sipped conferencewater and conferred. After a modicum of tedium you shattered the boredom abruptly. You stood up—to avoid being interrupted—and quit. But not without first challenging the graphs the President of the Board of Directors presented, citing contrary evidence that our parent company had not been "affected by" the so-called "quote recession unquote" and was actually profiting more than ever as a result of closing factories in America and opening them in Central America, South Africa, and the Soviet Union where labor could be more easily mistreated. You spoke for fifteen minutes and ended with a flourish. The audible silence was punctuated only by the President sipping his cool water coolly. I was aghast and even a little flabbergasted. I couldn't believe how stupid you were. We waited. If you quit, you were going to lose your job for sure! You stared across your clipboard unblinking. How could you afford to do that? A pin dropped in the next room. What could be more important than routine entrenchment in an uncomfortable position for money? The President cleared her throat. My index finger coiled on the shutter waiting to expose the film as soon as the tiniest sign of a worried frown crossed the President's unjovial countenance. We would make front page again for sure with our journalistic prowess. We were a crack investigative team. You asked the questions and I photographed the reactions. You utilized penetrating insight and I pushed a tiny button. You researched the increasingly murderous nature of the "Global Economy" and I pushed a really tiny button. As she opened her mouth to reply there came an eruption of bulbs. "Hey!" she cried "don't photograph me with my mouth open." But it was too late, I had just taken my 100th consecutive bad driver's license photo. It was a pathetic satisfaction I derived from this job but the only one. Cheerfully, I peeled off the negative and walked behind the counter to have the photo laminated. Maybe a few mispellings to top it off: How's life in Sarasoda, Lamont Perkinsl? Another State of Florida license stamped **<u>Under 21</u>** in bold red letters (even though your 21st birthday was less than a month away. (oh well (rules are rules (chuckle)))). Whistling, I walk out and present you with your license as well as the usual forms for you to fill out as well as a couple of unusual forms too. Anything to delay the moment you slide your newly-unrevoked-for-speeding-in-anger license into your wallet and storm the exit in a cold thanks of aggravated gratitude and speed home. You were number 37 and we are up to number 345 now. Bye now. After work I went over to you for a couple drinks. You always were my favorite bar. Sitting on a stool with my boot on your brass rail, I felt deep contentment. Because staring at my reflection in your Dewars mirror, drinking your cold Double Diamond, smoking my Camel, it felt as though poisoning my body were the dignified act of a gentleman. I told your bartender the joke about the Hard Science Restaurant in which a customer complains because her glass is liquid to which the waitress responds "Yes madam all our crystal is noncrystalline." He didn't get it so I began to finish drinking. Later that morning I was in the kitchen watching the sun rise cooking yesterday's breakfast of sundriedtomatoes with shiitakemushrooms when my housemate Andy wandered in sleepily, up for work. "I've finally done it!" I cried. "What?" he yawned. "I've gone around the clock backwards and met you coming from the other direction. You lapped me. You're a day older now." "Oh" Andy replied and cracked an egg on the edge of a skillet on a burner next to the burner on which my skillet resided in which the shrimp simmered in a sheen of butter in which grated parsley was. I had been up for two weeks and was quite extroverted. "Andy you should be eating more pineapple. I hear that if you don't eat enough pineapple you get this disease where you break out in barklike scales and in the advanced stages you get a frond on top of your head." He ran his fingers through his hair blushing. Andy fried an omelet while I grated Romano. He poured his morning juice while I opened my nightly Sheaf Stout. At moments like these I felt Andy and I were really in tune. At the same instant we both moved toward the stereo, I to play something abrasive and rudimentary with singing and he to play something pleasant and complex without, at the same instant an instant later we both froze, retreated in timid politeness and polite timidity. We both apologized at the same time, then silence, then both apologized at the same time for interrupting, then silence. After that we seldom spoke. I was in the Autumn of my years, he in the Spring of his. We were the vernal and autumnal equinoxes destined to remain on opposite sides of the sun. He was my housemate and I had to tell him that the woman around whom I had built successive nonrecurrent segued fantasies in which first and second person pronouns were used almost at the expense of their antecedents in order that the point of view might be transferred from the abstract to the concrete to the historical to the scientific to the silly was coming to sleep in his house, but I didn't know how to break it to him. Do you ever fantasize about having an awkward conversation with someone? I passed him the peppermill and casually mentioned "By the way, a strange woman will be living in the house in one week. I'm sorry I mean unfamiliar, she's not really strange. Well, come to think of it, I can see how you might think she is..." Then over morning and evening coffee he didn't seem to mind and told me about how he got a summer job working the graveyard shift at the Stanford Linear Accelerator Center. They keep the accelerator running all night, smashing electrons into antielectrons nonstop. Andy had to watch over it and make sure nothing went wrong. He couldn't rest until vast amounts of aggregated data confirmed electroweak theories. This is the link between the electrical and weak forces upon which the Grand Unified Theories (except they can't explain human behavior) will be built. Andy knew that if there was a connection between the electrical and weak forces, on a superatomic level it probably wasn't responsible for much except when your car won't start. Andy stared at the readouts through dry tired eyes ingesting vendingmachine coffee from styrofoam. Waiting for the Z^0 (Z-naught). Z^0, like me, is its own antiparticle. Andy was forbidden to blink because any existing Z^0 would quickly decay into a bottomquark and an antibottomquark—

Z^0_bb .

—which is not really a bottomquark, its just bottomflavored. Top and bottom, truth and beauty. Andy was trying to get from the bottom of his thoughts to the top and kept ending up in the anti-bottom instead. That Summer would find Andy finding himself trying to unravel the secrets of the universe while being entangled in a academic bureaucracy. His attempts to define the cosmos by a few simple rules was being impeded by a University with many elaborate ones. The closer Andy came to finding an explanation for existence the more difficult it became to define himself in terms of research grants. He felt he was losing his strangeness and charm. His mind whirled like an electron in a Hydrogen atom whose orbit traces a spherical nonpolar charge. In his dreams he was Z^0 being pursued by the United States Military. He careened through the microcosm trying to find a safe place to decay into a bottom quark and antibottomquark. He woke up in the description of the destruction of surplus value in an open copy of *Das Capital* at the accelerator console. Andy was having an induced dipole moment and didn't notice the blinking red light at first. An antielectron had escaped and Andy had to go looking for it with a flashlight in dark unused corridors in the basement. He had to be very careful not to step on it or it would be annihilated. He lost his way walking deeper and deeper into the workings of the accelerator. The flashlight didn't seem to be working. No light could escape. It was then that Andy realized he was travelling at the speed of light. He had wandered into the accelerator by mistake. Andy and the antiAndy disappeared in a blinding invisible flash of Xrays. The strings crescendo. Romeo and the antiRomeo cross rapiers and both disappear. Or something like that. The point ive been trying to get at is that someday i would like to do a production of Romeo and Juliet with a different ending um do you know how the play ends like Juliet takes this fake poison right which only kills her for a little while or something like that anyway Romeo barges into like her tomb right and he sees her lying there and thinks shes like dead right but she isnt hes only like asleep or unconscious or something i dont know yknow but anyway like then Romeo kills himself by ingesting a poisonous substance but like in my production okay he ingests fake poison right so then when Juliet wakes up and sees him lying there like asleep right she kills herself too but like she ingests fake poison too so like then a couple of hours go by then like Romeo wakes up and sees like yknow Juliet kinda lying there and he goes wow man shes dead id better kill myself again and then a couple more hours go by and then when the audience starts getting sorta restless Juliet like yeah you got it wakes up and discovers Romeo and then the whole thing uh repeats like one of those thingamajiggers whatchamacallit thingamabobs... loops. For days. Long after the audience has left and stopped coming back on subsequent nights to see if anything has happened yet. I've even figured out how I can finance a production which lasts forever and only seats an audience once. I can't believe nobody thought of this before. All I do is get a creditcard, use it to get a cash advance, deposit the cash in my checking account, and use it to pay my monthly creditcard installments. Have you heard about creditcards? They're great. You go to buy something and the creditcardcompany actually pays for it. I have no idea how they stay in business. And they actually gave me one. When you arrive in six days we can charge lots of stuff. We can fill a wading pool with lime sherbet and go snorkeling. Let's find a jacuzzi with jets of steam. Then we can make a cappuccino whirlpool bubblebath. I will sprinkle whitechocolate shavings while you splash in the smooth froth of milk. My creditcardcompany recently bought me a dehumidifier to celebrate the quincentennial anniversary of the invention of interest rates, whatever those are. I wrote them a thankyou note, including the postscript "suckers!" The humidity in Illinois is such that the very word "humidity" will inspire a grave nod from anyone who has ever lived here including you. My basement is like dry ice cream now. When I first plugged my dehumidifier in I turned it up too high and all my property was freezedried. Tiny mounds of colored powder sat where each possession once was. I eyedrop a drop of water on one of them and it turns back into a chair. The rest of my stuff I am sweeping into envelopes. I am labeling and sealing each one carefully. A record collection weighing approximately a ton (rounding up to the nearest ton) will now fit inside a manila envelope. Everything I own is alphabetized inside a filing cabinet. This is proving to be an excellent system of organization. My basement is less cluttered than ever. No more moving and storage costs. I am liberated from the material weight of a lifetime of reckless conspicuous consumer overspending as well as my neurotic obsession with furniture rearrangement ("Buckminster Fuller would have put the endtable here") as long as it never floods. Luckily, as I may have mentioned, I live in a basement and basements never flood. Enclosed in this letter is a freezedried waterbed: just add water twice. I love my dehumidifier. It is the most expensive disposable commodity I've ever owned. It is one of those outrageously expensive useless consumer goods I will never again be able to survive without. Living as well as I do on my income is like juggling, and sometimes lemons limes and oranges roll all over the stage. The audience, filled with my creditors and their children, boo and fling tomatoes. I grin sheepishly, bells and scepter, exit lease left. I lie in bed all morning trying to conserve my angular momentum, waiting for the next workshift, waiting for death, delirium, a meal... I am not winning any bread. I am not bringing home any bacon. I am not putting any food on the table. How will I earn enough to feed you as well as you deserve while still procrastinating my destiny with capitalism by struggling to avoid the career which will usurp my identity as it has the others? I want to sauté my bell peppers using only Extra Virgin Olive Oil but am afraid I will slide between the gears and be chewed up, be destroyed like family and friends who fell from being people to being professionals as they fell from having jobs to having careers. As long as I am below the poverty level I can look up and see the workings of the machine. As it runs me over. Over. I read you loud and clear. Over. We have invented the telephone. You were in the other room when I called "Lamont, come here... I miss you." You were on the otherside of the bulletproof glass and we spoke through a phone line being monitored by guards. You were telling me that you had baked a typewriter inside the cake you brought for me so I would finally have a weapon. I wasn't sure how to shush you. The guards played pinochle with headphones on. They could have been listening to any of the other prisoners or Mantovani. Also there were extra ribbons in the cupcakes. "What about paper?" I whispered as quietly as I could... You looked disappointed, as though you had forgotten, then your eyes rebrightened. "I'll mail you some." I cherished these moments when I could see your face divided into a grid of rhomboids by the wires in the bulletproof glass and hear your voice crackle through the tinny tiny speaker. While I was a political prisoner, especially after the lockdown, I lost all contact with the outside world, which was collapsing in on itself. Evidence of this can be seen today in any toy store. Legos are an indicative social indicator. In addition to the fact that nowadays most elaborate and expensive lego sets consist of only two or three elaborate and expensive lego pieces which can only be combined in two or three simple and cheap ways; there are three recent lego developments which conclusively prove that we are in trouble: 1. Lego people with facial hair can no longer be construed as female. 2. Lego waiters—while I grew up with the lego lunar lander and dreamed of becoming an astronaut, today's children can dream of working in a restaurant, or becoming 3. a lego visigoth. That's right, medieval lego barbarians are preparing children for the collapse of law and order as they play invade plunder siege sack rape and pillage. I led an extremely sheltered life in Marion maximum security prison. To change the subject, you began to tell me about your summer job working for the Florida Dental Exam board. There was a large auditorium filled with young dentists and at the front a slide projector displayed slides of teeth horribly disfigured by diseases the aspiring young dentists had a minute to identify. Your job was to walk around and make sure none of them cheated by looking inside one another's mouths with tiny mirrors. But, you explained in a burst of static, you found it hard to avoid looking at the slides: enormous images of chipped shattered decaying bleeding discolored disfigured teeth and gums. Slide number 21: partial cleft palate. You chuckled. That was an easy one.

Even though you had not been to medical school yet you felt you could outscore any of the young aspirants due to actual experience. Slide number 22: gum rot. I scribbled hastily in my exam booklet as you strode quietly by. Cause: rotting gums. Symptoms: rotting gums. Treatment: prevent the gums from rotting. Scribble scribble scribble. I could almost smell the newly refinished interior of my own waiting room with back issues of *Good Housekeeping*. I could see shrinkwrapped toothbrushes inscribed William Gillespie, DDS. There was a 15minutebreak during which I flossed in a courtyard of palms and pelicans. During the second part of the exam we were all given a plaster teeth simulacrum upon which we were to perform a simulated root canal. Two rows in front of me, a student began rubbing her jaw and moaning. It seems she had bit down on her pen too hard and fractured a crown. You made your way down the aisle and peered inside her mouth. Hmmm... Easy enough. You called for novocaine. As I watched you perform the operation I fantasized that you were giving me mouthtomouth resuscitation. You tilted my head back, repositioned my tongue, removed any obstructing material, pinched my nose closed... and my lungs filled with the fragrance of your exhalations. Carbon dioxide, residual oxygen, water vapor. I woke up kissing my pillow, my mouth full of feathers. What embarrassing things had I murmured to you in my sleep? You were the German language and I found your gendered nouns and multiple secondpersonpronouns at first uninviting. But your tendency to combine your capitalized compoundnouns including numbers such as nineteenhundredthre eandninety fascinated me. How can I tell you? I want to study the bacteria that aid your digestion. I want to learn the microscopic mites who feed on microscopic flakes of your dead skin. I want to investigate the fleas your cats bring you. I want to attend to your needs on a microscopic level, feeding each cell with an eyedropper, one by one, removing the wastes. I wish I knew you when you had mono nucleosis. I had mono nucleosis too. We could have lain on adjacent sofas rasping while waves of exhaustion buffeted us. By the way, what are you doing on New Years Eve 1999? Well, if you're not doing anything I'm not doing anything either so maybe we could, um, not do anything together. I mean, do nothing together. I mean, do something together. Well, I don't know what exactly. I know: let's go to a restaurant. I know this exquisitely weird place in Spain. Dali's: the Surrealist Restaurant. The waiters wander through balancing crumbs of Portuguese bread and strange wineglasses on their palettes. They inscribe orders on easeled canvas using fanshaped brushes which flicker like a hummingbird's wings. They are besieged by complaints from every table. Excuse me there's no gravity at this table. My knife is spinning and I'm afraid to get near it. Excuse me I ordered the Enigma of Hitler. Is this all I get? Three beans and a tiny photograph of Hitler? Excuse me on the side of my plate there's a live bat tugging at this rubbery thing. Is that garnish? Excuse me I can't drink my coffee because its suspended by an inexplicable appendage five meters long. Excuse me I can't eat my food because my plate is scalding hot and ten meters across. Excuse me for interrupting but are you ready to order? Would you care to order for the gentleman? There, at Dali's, in the noncannibalism section, where, for our entertainment, a grand piano is being sodomized by the apparition of Lenin, we can toast our friendship with melting glasses. And then I will tell you how I will build my empire. I am going to open a restaurant. Its spraypainted sign will read "le Trough." It will be a long room with a rusty aluminum trough around the wall at about waist height through which will sluice a brown juice which consists of partially pureed ingredients selected on the basis of affordability for example old produce a grocerystore would otherwise have to throw away or buckets of scraps scraped by dishwashers off of plates in other restaurants sold to us as edible waste at pennies a bucket. Le Trough would open its doors for an hour every noon and a wave of businessmen would trample in, rudely shoving one another aside to immerse their shaven faces white shirts and floral ties in the brown swill, lapping greedily. And you would look at me kind of funny. "Don't worry" -I am a little offended- "we'll hose it down every night." I can already remember getting ready for that date that hadn't yet happened. The doorbell rang just after the final chord of Gustav Mahler's Symphony number five in C-sharp

78

minor and I wondered how long you had been waiting outside. I quickly adjusted my tophat, brushed off my spats, tightened my cummerbund, loosened my bowtie, polished my cufflinks, grabbed my cane, feared that I might appear selfconscious, changed into jeans and Tshirt, and opened the front door. You smiled and when I saw your face for the first time in fivepointfive months I still couldn't remember what you looked like. You were wearing that dress, you know, the one with the periodic table of elements. Or was it the one with the tessellation of Escherlizards?

"How did you get here?" I wondered aloud.

"Hmmm? Oh—bike." I looked—you had spoken truth. Your trusty 2wheeler leaned against a tree outside. ...I guess I'm riding on your handlebars to Gesundheit... Oh well, worry about that later. You arrived just in time because a cold wind was whipping up an electrical snow rain hail sleet storm. July in Illinois was proving to be about as reliable as December, which melted. But you had remembered to bring Summer Solstice Tropic of Cancer sunshine and turned it on indoors. Dinner was ready. I wasn't sure what to wear so as we ate I excused myself to change clothes every five minutes, reemerging as a cowboy one moment, spaceman the next, trying really hard to look as though I paid no attention to my appearance. You had turned over my letters to reveal me hiding beneath and the sunlight was blinding.

Here was the menu I proposed:

mozzarella parmigiano ricotta spinach calzone asparagus
mushroom wholewheat pasta creamy bechamel prosciutto
mushroom lasagna marinara fettucine with black olive puree and
artichokes vegetarian cumin cilantro lime burritos

:I wanted you to think I was six parts Italian and one part Brazilian. Finally after you had eaten all seven courses and dessert (Zabaglione) and after dinner drinks and coffee I brought out the

79

Parodi cigarillos and we puffed in complacency, me occasionally hacking. I wondered if I should kiss you. I wasn't sure how to communicate my apprehension at this instinctive pleasure but socially reinforced inevitability. Should I suddenly dash my chair into bits and set it aflame to make smoke signals for you? Possessed by an uncomfortable mixture of the courtship dance of the subantarctic wandering albatross (Diomedea exulans) and *Romeo and Juliet* (Act II, scene ii. The former ends when both stand face to face with necks stretched and wings open, the latter ends when Romeo and Juliet kill themselves as a final demonstration of their crippling emotional and sexual codependency). I knelt beside you. When our parted lips were one angstrom apart the scream of a circularsaw came from the attic with a rain of sawdust. It was my housemate Andy and his lab partners—the Hovercraft Guys—building a more effective propulsion system. I blinked the sawdust from my eyes and looked deeply into your safety goggles. You reached for your breathing mask but the phone was already ringing. I answered it. It was my floor manager Marykay asking me to come into work in halfanhour. "Hold on," I stalled, "there's a call on the otherline." It was the sound of your dad loading his shotgun. "Ich kann daB nicht verstehen" I stalled. I hung up and the circularsaw cut through its own cord and there followed a descending whine and a period of silence. "Maybe we should go for a walk instead" I offered. You agreed. You lay a briefcase on the table and opened it. It was filled with Gainesville mushrooms, frosted with glittering crystalline psilocybin. Their rounded caps undulated in the hallucinogenic vapor rising from their midst where a lizard flicked its tongue at a fairy. "My favorite." I thanked her. What would happen to the letter after we dosed? Love William.

P.P.S. Dear Lamont a little old lady left me a nice tip at the restaurant today: $100,000 all in a neat brick of nonsequential hundreds. As I finish this postscript, my bags are already packed and waiting by the door and my planetickets are in my vest pocket. I guess this is goodbye. Come visit me in Mexico City. I'll be living on somebody's roof I'm sure. Well, you take care now, take care of Florida and all our friends down there. Oh, and tell Professor Bergren for me that the Latent Contextualization of Excrescent Circumlocution is Tantamount to the Postfrustration Phase of the Industrial Development of Snack Cakes which are actually, if you can read through the cutesy phonetic missspelllllings on the wrapper, "chocolate-flavored" instead of chocolate. I've always wanted to tell him that but never had the guts. Even when we worked as travelling cinderblock salesmen in the 30s. The 1830s, by the way, before the invention of horses. I wonder if his back is still bothering him? That reminds me: I saw Giroux the other day. He came to my signing at the Postfuturist bookstore and asked me to autograph my latest bestseller (*Erecting Divisions: What Comes after Postmodernism?*) for his **Mom**. I couldn't believe how shy that guy was. I jabbed his ribs and called him a homophobe just to show that there was no hard feelings but he blushed and left without paying for the book. I decided not to chase him down—anybody else and I would have—but I felt sorry for the guy. Ever since Michael Dyson threw him out of the band and started making solo albums. Well my flight leaves in twelve minutes and, since I live in the penthouse apartment of the Air-Traffic Control Tower, I guess I have about five more minutes to kill. Which gives me just enough time to get sentimental without explaining my emotions. You, Lamont, are the one who set off signal flares in my left ventricle before I could warn you that that's where I store explosives in the wintertime. You are the one who opened a can of catfood for me when I did figureeights around your ankles, and I refuse to believe that it was because I wouldn't stop meowing. You are the one whose dulcimer and impossible-to-decipher Irish folk music absolves me of the responsibility of having to write letters in whose sentences I am forced to dwell on the disappointing consistency of my own perceptual reality. You are a hallucination far better than any of mine. You have provided me with a key to my own weirdness, and this overwrought postpostpostscript is such a testimony. My heart is a fourchambered organ which plays minor chords in your absence. I have 88 keys but the full range of my emotions is less than a halfstep. Won't you accept my microtonal intervals? Well that's enough. Gotta go. When I get to Mexico City maybe I'll open a cantina whose battered wooden sign is ornamented with a handpainted depiction of you surrounded by roses which will peel and flake in the ruthless equatorial glare. I guess I never was very good at goodbyes. Or hellos for that matter. And how are yous? I hate those. How am I what? How is it going where? Look up and see for yourself. I'm okay at I'll be right back, but that's about it. In closing, I would like to share with you the words of a departed colleague of mine, Orville Thrump, when he said: "Eggwhites should be beaten into stiff peaks." That was the last thing he said to me before the bizarre eggbeater accident that caused him to lose his tenure. In his letters to Annabelle Smith dated the same month, he confesses: "Try as I might I can't keep the alfredo sauce from boiling." These foreboding words tell of Thrump's realization of his impending fall. Even then, he was relying heavily on sandwiches and his typetoken marinara which was suspected by many historians to include carrots, an ingredient Thrump himself had scoffed at while still at Moosewood. Indeed, a grocery list dated May 18th makes no mention of garlic. It reads:

Heinz 57 sauce
Kraft Macaroni
Lil'Dabney Snack Cakes
beer

Clearly this is not the grocerylist of a self-proclaimed "truly remarkable genius." During this time period Thrump confessed to me of a "gnawing hunger" which he refused to believe was caused by hunger. He would go for days without flossing and spoke wildly of plans to open a Mexican restaurant. Did I mention that I was going to Mexico City? Everything is fine with us there. The weather there is sunny. Wish you were there. I can hear the boat trumpet its horns to announce boarding time. This is Aloha for me. I plan to take a cruiseship from Illinois to New Orleans (which will disembark in Memphis and Nashville) and then I will rent a car and drive across the Gulf of Mexico—I've always wanted to do that. I will probably have to swim to get inland as far as Mexico city. I'm walking out the door right now and realize with a sniff that I left the oven on and the pilot light isn't lit. All four burners of the gas stove are on high. Furthermore, I forgot to turn off the faucets when I filled the bathtub an hour ago. I also forgot my wallet containing the bustickets. Good thing I caught it in time so I could remember to leave the door ajar with my keys dangling from the lock. Sayonara.

Letter to Lamont. First Spineless Edition. 2005.
ISBN 0-9724244-5-8. $10.
Text © William Gillespie.
Cover image: "Waking From a Dream" © Scott Westgard.

SPINELESS BOOKS  PROVIDENCE, RI

www.ingramcontent.com/pod-product-compliance
Lightning Source LLC
Chambersburg PA
CBHW031858170626
46807CB00004B/1782